Are you suffering from the SMART
<u>WOMAN'S</u>
<u>EXCESSIVE</u>
<u>EATING</u>
<u>TRAP?</u>

- Do you worry about your weight even though many people tell you that you look trim?
- Are you upset by even small increases in your weight?
- Do you set high standards for yourself—or do you (or others) think of you as a perfectionist?
- Do you use food to lift your spirits when you feel stressed or depressed?
- Do you try to be all things to all people?
- Do you fluctuate between periods of sensible eating and exercise and unhealthy eating and erratic exercise?
- Does overeating or weight gain lower your confidence in family, work, or social relationships?

What Drives You To Succeed Could Be Driving You To Overeat!

If you don't eat the way you want to—and haven't been able to change—this book is for you. Written by two leading experts in the field, it draws on psychological insights, life-style strategies, and actual behavioral exercises to help active career women end food cravings and destructive eating habits—in just 12 days!

Also by Peter M. Miller, Ph.D.

*The Hilton Head Metabolism Diet**
*The Hilton Head Executive Stamina Program**
Selfwatching (with Ray Hodgson, Ph.D.)
Personal Habit Control
Alternatives to Alcohol Abuse
(with Maria Mastria, Ph.D.)
Behavioral Treatment of Alcoholism

*Published by
WARNER BOOKS

IF I'M SO SMART, WHY DO I EAT LIKE THIS?

PETER M. MILLER, PH.D.
HOWARD RANKIN, PH.D.

WARNER BOOKS

A Warner Communications Company

This Warner Books Edition is published by arrangement with
Rawson Associates, a division of Macmillan Publishing Company,
866 Third Avenue, New York, N.Y. 10022.

Cover design by Tom Tafuri

Warner Books, Inc.
666 Fifth Avenue
New York, N.Y. 10103

Ⓦ A Warner Communications Company

Printed in the United States of America

First Warner Books Printing: November, 1989

10 9 8 7 6 5 4 3 2 1

To Gabrielle and Francesca

CONTENTS

Chapter 1

INTRODUCING SWEET—

The Smart Woman's Excessive Eating Trap

*I*f you are an intelligent, active, ambitious, and self-demanding woman who takes pride in being in control of her life, you may very well suffer in silence with an eating problem that is specific to busy women like yourself who have certain personality traits in common.

This heretofore undescribed syndrome is characterized by eating behavior that fluctuates between healthy eating and exercise on the one hand and brief episodes of overeating and erratic exercise on the other. It's a classic case of Dr. Jekyll and "Ms." Hyde, in which you may feel extremely confused by such paradoxical eating behavior.

This book will describe what we call the Smart Woman's Excessive Eating Trap (SWEET), explain why you eat this way, and, most important of all, outline a 12-day program to enable you to free yourself from this eating problem. Through our clinical work with hundreds of women at the world-famous Hilton Head Health Institute, we are happy to be able to share our understanding and clinical expertise with you.

Before we get into more detail, let's take a closer and more personal look at one woman's experience with the Smart Woman's Excessive Eating Trap.

Carol's Hidden Dilemma

Carol is a 32-year-old woman who leads a very active career, family, and social life. She is married to Jim and has two children, Jennifer, age six, and Eric, age four. On the homefront, Carol also has to contend with Jezebel, a lovable but frisky golden retriever, Mittens, a stray calico cat whom Jennifer adopted on her way home from school one day, six goldfish, and a canary! Car pools, household chores, and school committees keep Carol on the go, not to mention the special meals she has to prepare for Eric, who has several food allergies.

Carol is as dedicated to her career as she is to her family. As a marketing consultant with an MBA from a top university, Carol and her husband run a small but rapidly growing marketing consulting firm. Their business requires a great deal of travel, with Carol and Jim alternating trips so one of them can be home with the children as often as possible. In one week alone, Carol traveled to Japan, Korea, and Hong Kong, representing her state's foreign trade commission.

As if this weren't enough, Carol volunteers at the local chapter of the American Cancer Society, planning special health programs and fund-raising events. Since her father died of stomach cancer five years ago, Carol feels a special need to devote some of her time to this cause.

Jim and Carol also lead an active social life. They enjoy small get-togethers with other young, successful couples. They realize that attending numerous social events in their community is not only pleasurable, but is essential for cultivating business relationships.

Ever since the birth of her children, Carol has had to fight a 15-pound overweight problem. This is especially frustrating to her, because she prides herself on her appearance. A slender, firm body and stylish clothing go hand-in-hand with her conviction that she should strive for the best in every aspect of life. To this end, Carol works hard at counting calories and getting exercise. She reads articles and books on dieting, nutrition, and physical fitness, and knows about carbohydrate loading, training heart rate, and lean body mass. As far as fitness is concerned, Carol does well for a time, sticking strictly to a diet, jogging four days a week with Jim, and attending an aerobic exercise class at a local athletic club three evenings a week. When she is "on" her diet and exercise program, Carol follows the rules faithfully. She is someone who exerts maximum effort in whatever she does. Jim sometimes takes her to task for being a perfectionist, wanting to do things "just so" and taking on more tasks than she should, simply because she knows she can do them better than anyone else. Yet Carol likes her life to run on a tight schedule. She is an all-or-nothing person who can be relied on to give 100 percent.

Between family, career, friends, travel, and volunteer work, however, Carol began to have difficulty keeping her life orderly and in balance. It's not that she disliked her busy life. She enjoyed the challenge of an active, multifaceted existence. But the stress of such a lifestyle was undeniable.

As with many women in her situation, Carol's "overload" problem manifested itself in eating difficulties. Carol, who normally was in control of her eating behavior, began to experience periodic eating binges. She found herself fluctuating between strict adherence to a diet/exercise program and careless abandon of all dietary rules. She would follow her nutrition and fitness plan religiously for several days and then suddenly would lose control, forsake her exercise, and eat sweets and "junk" food. This out-of-control eating behavior was so alien to her basic personality that its occurrence confused and frustrated her.

Carol couldn't understand her behavior. Usually she was very rational in her approach to life. Her physical appearance was important to her. Yet she was experiencing increasingly frequent episodes of what she referred to as "mini-binges." She either was "on" her diet or "off" it. There was never any middle ground. She seemed to be turning into a person of extremes.

Carol was so disturbed by this eating behavior that she discussed it only once, with a close friend of hers. She realized that her husband knew what was going on, but she tried to hide it even from him. Frequently, she would raid the freezer for ice cream late at night, after Jim was asleep and the house was (finally!) quiet.

When Carol first consulted us at the Hilton Head Health Institute, she was guilt-ridden, depressed, and 18 pounds overweight. Her on-again, off-again eating problem was affecting her confidence and self-esteem. In fact, the title of this book was borrowed from Carol's plea to us during her very first session: "If I'm so smart, why do I eat like this?"

Fortunately, Carol successfully completed our 12-day Hilton Head Program and now, five years later, continues to be free of her negative eating behavior. She was relieved to find that not only did we understand her problem, but we had a solution to it.

Carol is only one of hundreds of cases that we have treated successfully. For the past 12 years we have been treating women with eating problems at the Hilton Head Health Institute on Hilton Head Island, South Carolina. Women from all over the world have consulted us and participated in our treatment programs. Now you, too, can benefit from our years of experience. Once and for all, you can be free of the Smart Woman's Excessive Eating Trap forever.

Before we go into more detail about our methods, let's take a closer look at the SWEET Syndrome so common among high-achieving women.

What Is the SWEET Syndrome?

The SWEET Syndrome refers to a seeming contradiction in behavior in which episodes of excessive eating afflict women who, from all outward appearances, appear to be very much in control of their lives. In fact, 80 percent of the time women with this problem count calories, avoid sugar and cholesterol-laden foods, load up on complex carbohydrates, and choose high-fiber breads and cereals. It's the other 20 percent of the time that this book is designed to help.

What Is an Out-of-Control Eating Episode?

During these episodes, your eating habits seem to be out of your control. Even though you know how to eat healthfully, you choose types and quantities of foods that you normally wouldn't touch. Rather than being driven to eat everything in sight, as a binge eater does, you may focus on one type of food or on one food group, such as sweets, fried foods, or breads and other starchy products.

Many of the women who enter our program are embarrassed and confused by these episodes. This eating seems so alien to their normal behavior. Many try to hide their problem from friends and family.

If these episodes describe you, you do have an eating problem, but you do *not* have what is generally termed an eating disorder. Unless you consistently binge and then force yourself to vomit, you do not have bulimia. Unless you are so obsessive about your weight that you are literally starving yourself, you do not have anorexia nervosa. And, unless you fluctuate between these two extremes, you do not have bulimarexia.

You may have read articles on eating disorders, and

because your symptoms sounded a little like the descriptions, you may have wondered if you were experiencing the early stages of a major eating problem. Your problem is most likely less severe. It is amazing that while the SWEET Syndrome is probably a more widespread problem than are eating disorders *per se,* this book is the first to describe this syndrome and to offer practical solutions.

The term "out-of-control eating" refers to a more general pattern than food bingeing. A food binge brings to mind the idea of eating everything in sight until nothing is left. While out-of-control eating can reach this extreme, it usually doesn't. Out-of-control eating is defined more in terms of *the feelings and experiences you have at the time rather than by the quantity or quality of what you are eating.* One of our clients, a 28-year-old television producer, described her feelings during one of these episodes:

"It was as if a strong force had taken over my mind and I was powerless against it. It was a horrible feeling. I hate to feel so weak and helpless and incapable of taking any action to make things right again. I'm usually such a take-charge person. The whole experience was very frightening to me."

During this episode, our client had consumed a total of three bagels with cream cheese! Hardly much of a binge, you might say. Exactly! It's the out-of-control *feeling* that's important, whether you eat three bagels or three dozen chocolate-covered doughnuts. In fact, you may even overeat such "healthy" foods as carrots, apples, whole-grain cereals and breads, and even bean sprouts! Remember, this is an eating problem, *not* a food problem.

9

Are We Describing You?

Could you be suffering from the Smart Woman's Excessive Eating Trap? While a more extensive test is provided in the next chapter, you may have this syndrome if you are:

- Between the ages of 21 and 50

- Orderly, oriented toward time and detail in your life

- Health- and weight-conscious

- Self-demanding

- Success-oriented

- Intelligent and well-educated

You Are Not Alone

Please keep in mind that you are definitely not alone. We have helped thousands of women eradicate the SWEET Syndrome. This book will help you understand this syndrome, how it originated, and why it continues. Most importantly, we will provide you with a step-by-step, easy-to-follow program designed to rid you of this eating problem forever.

After years of extensive clinical investigation both in Great Britain and the United States, we have formulated a treatment that *will* work for you. One of us, Dr. Peter Miller, was already well known in the United States for establishing and directing the Hilton Head Health Institute, an internationally recognized health retreat located on Hilton Head Island, South Carolina. While helping thousands of men and women achieve healthier and happier lives, the Institute has been especially noted for the development of innovative weight-control techniques. Dr. Miller's bestselling book *The Hilton Head Metabolism Diet* broke new ground on the issue of metabolism and weight loss. More recently, the Hilton Head Health Institute has been noted for breakthrough executive health and stamina programs aimed at hard-driving career men and women. Dr. Miller's popular book *The Hilton Head Executive Stamina Program* enables busy executives to regulate their nutritional, fitness, and stress needs in practical ways that do not interfere with the hectic pace of the business world.

The second half of our team, Dr. Howard Rankin, enjoyed an equally illustrious reputation in Great Britain for his work in the field of addictions and eating disorders. Prior to joining forces with Dr. Miller at the Hilton Head Health Institute, he was known internationally as an expert on health psychology based on his clinical research work at the University of London's prestigious Addiction Research Unit as well as at St. Andrew's Hospital, one of Britain's largest private hospitals.

During a NATO-sponsored conference in Norway at which we both were speakers, we enthusiastically shared our experiences and ideas about eating problems. Over the next several years we continued to examine these problems in our patient populations in the United States and Great Britain. Transatlantic collaborative research followed, which led to the development of exciting treatment techniques that we tested in our respective clinical facilities.

Before long, we realized that, in order to develop a comprehensive treatment for the SWEET Syndrome, we had to unify and intensify our efforts. It was at that point that we joined forces at the Hilton Head Health Institute and developed what was to become a major advance in the understanding and treatment of eating problems in women.

Since that time, our progress has been rapid. Our backgrounds as clinical psychologists with more than 20 years' experience in the fields of food abuse, addiction, and executive health—combined with our counseling of thousands of women who have come to the Hilton Head Health Institute from all over the world—have enabled us to develop an effective, yet easy-to-follow program of hope. It is the only eating program that takes your particular personality and lifestyle as a smart, busy woman into account.

A Major Breakthrough: The Hilton Head 12-Day Program

The result of our efforts is the Hilton Head 12-Day SWEET Program. Our goal was to compress a complete, comprehensive treatment program into 12 days for maximum effectiveness.

The case of Carol mentioned above will give you a brief idea of how we attack the SWEET Syndrome. We worked with Carol over a 12-day period and taught her the secrets of the Hilton Head plan. She first learned our techniques of rebalancing her life so that she was neither overly perfectionistic nor lackadaisical. Carol now has a new kind of control over her life in which she is able to structure her career and personal life *but also keep enough time for herself*. By following the Lifestyle Balancing Module of our treatment plan, Carol was able to increase her sense of personal freedom while maintaining a busy life.

Carol's perfectionistic thinking patterns were modified by means of our Cognitive Change Module. In this phase of treatment we performed an in-depth analysis of Carol's thinking patterns (a technique you will be learning to accomplish on your own) and then helped her record audiotapes of new, less constrictive thought patterns. Through repeated practice with these tapes, she began to reprogram her mind. We concentrated especially on thoughts and feelings that, in the past, had triggered undesirable eating episodes.

Finally, we put Carol through our Craving Control Ladder Module. Using this module, her body and mind were deconditioned and desensitized to the thought and sight of foods that were high on her craving list. This phase of treatment required her actually to look at, touch, and even taste foods that were most associated with out-of-control eating. In the beginning, such exposure to food occurred under "neutral" emotional conditions. As treatment progressed, she was exposed to these foods while she was tired or otherwise "off guard" in order to simulate the conditions that normally triggered her eating. During this deconditioning process, Carol gained more and more strength and control over food.

Carol's is a true success story. After she returned home we followed her case very closely. She lost a total of 20 pounds and maintains an ideal weight of 120 pounds. She now leads a richer, more balanced life. She continues to be a successful career woman, wife, and mother, but is also a happier, healthier person. She has not experienced a single out-of-control eating episode in the past five years. She has broken the chains of this eating problem and is finally free.

We can help you just as we helped Carol. A new life is waiting for you—a balanced life in which food no longer rules your life. You will be, once and for all, your own person: slender, fit, and free from the SWEET Syndrome forever!

Chapter 2

ARE YOU CAUGHT IN THE SMART WOMAN'S EXCESSIVE EATING TRAP?

*W*e use the following quiz with our clients at the Hilton Head Health Institute to determine the extent of their involvement with the SWEET Syndrome. It will help you profile your own patterns of behavior toward food.

The SWEET Syndrome Quiz

On a sheet of paper, write "Yes" or "No" to each of the following questions. If your response falls somewhere in the middle on a question, try to decide whether it is more often "Yes" than "No" or vice versa.

1. Do you worry about your weight even though you receive assurances that you look trim?

2. Do you frequently read magazine articles and books on health, nutrition, and fitness?

3. Do you set very high standards for yourself?

4. Do you try to be all things to all people?

5. Do you (or others) think of yourself as a perfectionist?

6. Do you use food to lift your spirits when you are depressed?

7. Do you experience times when you feel almost driven to eat?

8. Do you fluctuate between periods of sensible, nutritious eating and out-of-control eating?

9. When your eating is out of control, do you sometimes have the feeling that someone or something has taken charge of your mind and body?

10. Do you fail to leave time in your schedule for activities for yourself, activities that you really enjoy?

11. Do you find it easier to control and structure your career and/or family than your own personal life?

12. Are you upset by even small increases in your weight?

13. Does either an episode of out-of-control eating or an increase in weight lower the confidence you feel in family, business, or social relationships?

Give yourself 10 points for each "Yes" answer and rate yourself on the scale below.

Total Score	SWEET Syndrome Category
90–130	Severe
50– 80	Moderate
20– 40	Mild
0– 10	None

If you scored 50 or above, you have a moderate to severe case of the SWEET Syndrome and can benefit from our treatment regimen. If you scored in the mild category, it may be that you are just now showing signs of this problem. Use of our treatment techniques will prevent any eating difficulties from worsening.

No matter how high your score, there is hope for you! This program will enable you to break the out-of-control eating cycle once and for all so that you can get on with the rest of your life.

Before you begin the program, Chapter 3 will provide a bit of mental preparation to help you benefit fully from the techniques we plan to share.

Chapter 3

UNDERSTANDING YOUR EATING STYLES

Your eating style varies according to your work environment and your personal habits. In subsequent chapters we will discuss in detail the psychology behind out-of-control eating, but in this chapter we are going to outline the typical eating styles, or behaviors, that characterize the SWEET Syndrome.

Four Key Environmental Factors

Our research reveals four work-related categories that influence the development of the SWEET Syndrome. Many people find that they have all of these influences in their careers—often at the same time!

Travel Having no set routine is one of the biggest difficulties for people attempting to control their eating habits. The disruption of travel is particularly acute for the busy woman because it combines a number of problematic elements.

First, there is trip preparation. This can be stressful, particularly if you feel the need to "clear your desk" and resolve all pending projects before you depart. Your return to the office following a trip also can be wearing as you face the prospect of catching up on events and handling material that has accumulated while you have been away.

Second, the act of traveling is also extremely demanding. Sitting too long in a pressurized airplane cabin leads to dehydration and fatigue. Waiting in airports can be frustrating. Changes in climate and time zones also require physical adaptation that takes time, meanwhile leaving a traveler vulnerable to fatigue and stress. Finally, the natural apprehension that accompanies a trip can make the 48 hours around the travel time extremely arduous. All of this occurs in addition to any concerns that you may have about the purpose of the trip and your performance upon arrival at your destination. June, an elegant ex-model from Connecticut, owns a management consulting firm with her husband. She accompanies him on several business trips a year. She has the important role during these trips of hosting cocktail parties and working with her husband to establish new contacts. At our first meeting she described a recent trip which encompassed all the difficulties inherent in business travel.

On this particular occasion, June and her husband were traveling from Hartford to Los Angeles, via Boston. Inclement weather delayed their morning arrival at the Hartford airport and they missed the commuter flight to Boston. They took the next flight out and after a frantic rush were able to make their West Coast connection with less than ten minutes to spare. By now it was lunchtime. After the stress of the morning, June was hungry and looking forward to lunch. However, because of the poor weather, the air traffic was backed up and their plane had to wait nearly an hour on the runway before it could finally take off. Lunch was served over two hours late. June had called ahead and asked for a special meal, always a useful tactic to consider when on long flights. Yet because she had asked for a special order, June was served last. She had ordered the vegetarian dish, hoping it would be low in calories. Unfortunately, the typical vegetarian dish served on airlines, while nutritious, contains a high amount of dairy products—particularly cheese—and therefore is not low-calorie. By this time June was not prepared to hassle and was happy just to settle for arriving in Los Angeles in one piece. June also knew that within two hours of arriving in L.A., she would be needing the energy to attend a large dinner and network with important clients. So she ate the meal served to her.

On arrival, June ran into further problems. She had no control over the menu choices for the cocktail party and subsequent dinner. June made the best of a difficult situation by putting into practice some of the coping strategies outlined in Chapter 18. But her experience highlighted the difficulties that travel can bring to those trying to maintain control over their diet.

Many people arriving at an unfamiliar place after a tiring journey are unprepared to search for restaurants that serve the healthy food to which they are accustomed. Eating sensibly during travel requires constant control, which is often difficult when you are stressed, fatigued, and have other pressing priorities. In Chapter 18 we will provide some tips on how to deal with travel and the following difficult situations.

Working Meals Business lunches, dinners, and working breakfasts present the career woman with other difficulties. These are mealtimes, so the chances are that you will be hungry and will want to eat something. Moreover, you probably will feel some social pressure to eat foods or drink alcohol in order to make your clients feel at ease, or to avoid offending others in your party. Third, your attention and concentration are directed toward implementing your agenda for the meeting. You simply may not have the requisite mental space to focus on the fine details of your nutritional choices and on tactics designed to limit your food intake.

Crucial Fact #1
Implementing strategies to control your
eating requires attention, concentration,
and preparation.

Business/Social Gatherings This category includes formal and informal dinners and cocktail parties. Here again, there are the problems of actually being hungry, feeling social pressure to eat and drink, and having large quantities of food readily available. Alcohol presents a real roadblock in the party situation. One of the effects of alcohol is to stimulate the gastric lining of the stomach, thereby creating feelings of hunger. This is precisely why alcohol is used as an aperitif. Alcohol also has a disinhibiting effect. This means that your best-laid plans can be sabotaged by a couple of drinks.

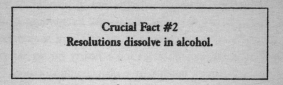

Crucial Fact #2
Resolutions dissolve in alcohol.

Meetings   Meetings at which food is available also present difficulties. Often, food is brought to the conference room because the meeting may extend through a mealtime. Once again, therefore, the chances are that you are hungry. Usually you have no choice about the type of food available. In certain meetings you might feel self-conscious about not eating when everyone else is, even though the food may not be to your liking. There will be times when you will have to eat because you know this might be your only opportunity to get some food for the next few hours. You might even be feeling light-headed and think that a boost to your blood-sugar level will bolster your concentration. The stress of the meeting and the effort required to focus on the issues at hand make it more difficult to exercise good control. What happened to Martha, an investment banker, on one particularly hectic day, highlights the difficulties inherent in this situation. Involved in a long lunchtime meeting, Martha eschewed the food that had been brought in to the meeting in favor of a banana and an apple. Martha spent the afternoon catching up on her work following the protracted meeting. She then rushed to a dinner party, deciding along the way to allow herself a cocktail but no pre-dinner snacks. About five minutes after she had finished her drink, Martha began to feel very fuzzy. Realizing that part of the problem was her empty stomach, Martha ate a plateful of hors d'oeuvres just before dinner was served. By avoiding alcohol for the rest of the evening and by drinking several large glasses of water, as well as eating a hearty dinner, Martha saved herself from a potentially embarrassing situation.

The situations mentioned above all influence your eating styles significantly. Our program is designed to help you deal with them. In later chapters we will detail specific techniques to handle these situations successfully.

Charting Your Personal Eating Style

Depending on your personal habits and the factors outlined above, you will exhibit at least one of three eating styles that we have identified in our clients. (It also is possible to possess the tendencies of more than one of these types.)

The Grazer   The Grazer is a person who rarely if ever gets to eat a proper meal, either by choice or circumstance. Instead of taking regular meals, the Grazer will snack periodically (sometimes incessantly) throughout the day. Often this eating style is adopted by a woman who does not like to leave her work to take regular meal breaks. When she does not have a working lunch scheduled, she will have snacks brought in to the office. While eating small, frequent meals can sometimes be a healthy alternative, particularly for those susceptible to rapid blood-sugar swings, grazing in this manner is generally unhealthy. For one thing, it is very difficult to keep track of exactly what and how much you have eaten, so the result is often too many calories of the wrong kind. Secondly, Grazers tend to indulge themselves in a variety of "goodies," from doughnuts to cookies, believing that they have not had a proper meal and therefore have calories to spare for such treats. This is a misconception that can lead to trouble. Take the case of Jennifer, who worked in the personnel department of a medium-size East Coast corporation.

Jennifer would start the day with only a cup of coffee for breakfast (like many people, she skipped breakfast in order to save some calories for later). After she had been at work for about an hour, she would feel hungry and would go to the cafeteria to buy a Danish pastry. She saw this as her breakfast. (You will already appreciate that Danish pastry is not the ideal breakfast food; it's high in sugar, which will lead to a blood-sugar slump later in the day.) Because Jennifer was a conscientious worker, she would stay in the office at lunchtime. This enabled her to meet with members of the work force during their lunch hour, a time preferable to them because it was less disruptive to their busy schedules. Frequently she met with colleagues in her office and had sandwiches brought in. The food usually included Jennifer's favorite—an ice-cream bar. Later in the afternoon, Jennifer would have another snack, typically a cookie or two. About three times a week Jennifer stayed late at the office, meeting with her superiors, networking with colleagues, or interviewing other members of the work force. On these occasions she would again send out for a snack—some pizza or a large sandwich from the local deli. At the end of such a day Jennifer would arrive home at about 8:30 P.M. An hour later she usually had a snack to "unwind," often some fruit with an occasional scoop of ice cream.

Jennifer's food intake does not appear excessive. She has not had a large meal during the day. Indeed, she has really had no full meal at all. She has not gorged herself uncontrollably. Yet at the end of the day, Jennifer has consumed nearly 2500 calories, eaten far too many foods high in simple sugars, and she has been mostly sedentary. It's hardly a surprise that she was gaining weight at a fairly rapid pace. The Conditioning Module of our Hilton Head Program helped Jennifer to change her eating habits.

Are you a Grazer? If you answer "true" to more than three of the five questions below, you may fit into this category.

1. I usually skip breakfast.
   TRUE   FALSE

2. I prefer to eat frequent snacks during the course of the day rather than full meals.
   TRUE   FALSE

3. I tend to eat while doing other things (e.g., in a meeting, in front of the TV, while working).
   TRUE   FALSE

4. I often indulge in "treats" during the day.
   TRUE   FALSE

5. I rarely go more than two hours without eating something.
   TRUE   FALSE

The Compensator   In contrast to Grazers, Compensators do eat regular meals, but do so to such an extent that they then feel guilty and try to compensate by eating nothing at all for the rest of the day, or even longer. The problem with this approach is that the subsequent restriction is so severe that it produces extreme hunger and deprivation. This sense of deprivation then results in an explosion of eating and even bingeing. Compensation creates more problems than it solves and only serves to perpetuate the overeating–guilt–deprivation–overeating cycle.

Gloria is a talent scout in California. Her day involved at least one working meal, typically lunch, and her career also involved a lot of traveling. She had decided that it was extremely difficult for her not to enjoy the full benefits of a substantial working lunch. She liked good food, wanted to make her clients feel at ease, and wanted to devote her full attention to the business at hand. So she would make her business lunch the one meal of her day. After lunch, she would eat no more that day to compensate for her large and fairly rich midday meal. The only problem was that by nine o'clock at night she was absolutely famished. She would try to hold out, but usually she would relent and have some chopped vegetables that she kept on hand in case of an emergency. When that failed to satisfy her, she would become very upset, decide that she was a complete failure at maintaining her weight, and work her way through the better part of half a gallon of ice cream. When she woke the next day, she was determined to eat nothing at all. This usually was not possible because she had scheduled another business lunch. Again she would vow just to eat lunch and nothing else. And so the pattern was repeated. Gloria justified this rather chaotic eating pattern by saying to herself that large lunches were the only way she could cope with the demands of her job. Of course, her eating actually was a function of how she handled food and had little to do with the fact that she conducted much of her work around lunch. The thinking patterns associated with this eating style are tackled in the Cognitive Change Module of the Hilton Head Program.

If you agree with at least three of the five questions listed below, you have strong Compensator tendencies.

1. I feel guilty if I feel full.
   TRUE   FALSE

2. I often will go hours without anything to eat.
   TRUE   FALSE

3. I prefer to eat regular meals.
   TRUE   FALSE

4. I often feel deprived of my favorite foods.
   TRUE   FALSE

5. I weigh myself at least three times a week.
   TRUE   FALSE

The Primer   Primers are similar to Compensators in that they often conduct their business over lunches and around food. Their difficulty is not the guilt and excessive restriction of the Compensator, however, but rather the fact that food seems to prime them for further eating. Once they have started eating, they find it difficult to stop.

Jan worked in the public relations division of a large Seattle corporation. Her job entailed some travel, occasional lunchtime meetings, and frequent cocktail parties. On days when Jan was able to control the time, place, and content of her own eating, she was fine. She would limit herself to regular but relatively small meals. When, however, she was at some official or work-related function, her day's diet went awry. A business luncheon would be the setting for her to eat a hearty meal that nearly always included dessert. By the middle of the afternoon she would experience a severe blood-sugar slump and feel the need to boost her flagging energy with cookies or pastry. Often, she then would go to a cocktail party and spend much of her time hovering near the buffet, snacking on the available goodies. Part of Jan's difficulty stemmed from the tension and performance anxiety surrounding business meetings. The tension made it extremely difficult for her to exercise control over her eating. The other major difficulty for her was that food really did create a desire for further eating, which she found irresistible. Using the Conditioning Module of our program, Jan was finally able to control this priming effect.

Three or more positive responses to the questions listed below indicate that you tend to be a Primer.

1. Once I start eating I find it difficult to stop.
    TRUE   FALSE

2. I find it difficult to exercise good control over my food intake during formal lunches and dinners.
    TRUE   FALSE

3. I am very tempted by sweet foods.
    TRUE   FALSE

4. I often have at least two glasses of alcohol with my main meal.
    TRUE   FALSE

5. I seem to put weight on very quickly.
    TRUE   FALSE

Later in this book we will outline specific techniques to deal with the foregoing situations using the Hilton Head Program. Now let's examine how these eating styles are shaped by certain thinking styles that govern your attitudes and behavior.

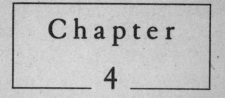

Chapter 4

THE QUEST
FOR
PERFECTION

*I*n our introductory chapter we profiled the three main components of the SWEET Syndrome. The first of these concerns your cognition, or thinking style. The notion of a thinking style may seem alien to you, but we have found that people's thinking can be categorized in much the same way as, for example, their handwriting.

What Are Thinking Styles?

At the heart of the SWEET Syndrome is a thinking style that is highly focused on maintaining control. It's certainly important to be effective in your life, but sometimes the need to be in control may be so strong that it ends up being counterproductive. It's simply not possible to control every detail in all the areas of life. In fact, people who are successful and exercise the most control in their lives do so by *accepting* the fact that they cannot control everything. They have learned to accept flexibility because they know that unreasonable demands—both on themselves and on others—cause anxiety and actually *undermine* good performance. To many achieving women, however, perfectionism seems natural and right. In the past, it may have helped them excel and reach the goals that have brought them success. This is why it is difficult to view perfectionism with objectivity.

We have found that women suffering from the SWEET Syndrome set far too stringent standards in their quest for excellence. This approach actually generates as much frustration and failure as it does success. It simply is not possible to take on all aspects of a complex life and expect to do them to perfection. Yet, failure is something that the person suffering from the Smart Woman's Excessive Eating Trap finds very hard to accept.

Crucial Fact #3
Rigid thinking leads to failure and frustration.

The secret of overcoming the SWEET Syndrome lies *not* in abandoning your attempts to gain control of your life, but in becoming more flexible and tolerant in certain areas. Our program will help you achieve this. It will help you to stop thinking in black and white and instead accept different shades of gray. All-or-nothing thinking is great when you get "all," but frustrating when you end up with nothing. One of the consequences of feeling frustrated or anxious is excessive eating. And one of the consequences of excessive eating is frustration at not being able to control your food consumption! This vicious cycle *can* be broken—that's our promise to you.

Frustration is a major cause of overindulgence not only in food, but in alcohol and drugs as well. It has not been our experience that women with this syndrome dabble much with drugs, although some undoubtedly do. We also have noted periodic excessive alcohol use that fell short of alcoholism in several of our clients. Frustration almost always led to excessive eating in the women that we have worked with. One reason for this is that women today—particularly career women—are understandably concerned with projecting a professional image and maintaining their appearance. Nearly all of them are watching their weight and restricting their food intake. Eating is therefore one area in which they are constantly exercising control. It is no surprise that such control will break down from time to time in response to stress, and that rigid dieting will be replaced with uncontrolled eating. These lapses result in frustration, which sets off even more eating!

Crucial Fact #4
Out-of-control eating is a response to a negative emotion such as frustration, anger, or stress. It has little to do with hunger.

In addition, eating is a very personal and private activity. Because eating can be done behind closed doors, it is one way to relinquish control in a "safe" setting. Sometimes, however, work situations or domestic obligations conspire to present women with both food and stress at the same time, and the SWEET Syndrome emerges into the open. How does this happen? To find out, let's examine the phenomenon of perfectionism.

The Five Causes of Perfectionism

The all-or-nothing thinking style that we have found to be linked to perfectionism is typified by the following comments:

"If I take on a job, I have to do it perfectly. I feel uncomfortable unless I can give myself ten out of ten. Actually, I have to give myself eleven out of ten to rest easy." Jan, a sales manager from the Midwest.

"I've always been committed to giving 1000 percent to everything I do. I will often work on a task until I know it can't be improved upon. I just hate that feeling that there is more I can do." Marlene, an administrator for a large West Coast company.

Many of our clients recognize the damaging effect this thinking style has on their lives. In fact, many had gone through expensive psychotherapy in an attempt to remedy the problem prior to coming to Hilton Head. Typically, such therapy brought interesting insights but did not materially alter their behavior. It's true that you DO have to work on identifying your thinking habits before you can change them. You just do not have to spend lots of time and money achieving these ends.

When we probed a little deeper, we found that there were five main reasons why our clients strived so hard to get straight A's in everything they did. If you see yourself in any of the five profiles that follow, it's vital to understand that you developed and maintained these thinking styles because they actually *helped* you cope successfully with many situations. You are not wrong or bad for having these thinking styles. Understand also that it is possible to fit into more than one of the profiles outlined below.

1. Distraction   The first group that we identified were women who felt comfortable only when there were projects to accomplish, with many commitments waiting in the wings and something constantly to occupy their minds. If they were not in this state, they felt very uneasy. They would get edgy and restless, and often would start nibbling food almost unconsciously. It seemed to us that attention to detail and thirst for work were motivated by a desire to distract themselves from other areas of life that were uncomfortable to think about. Although they were very successful at work, often they were tired and preoccupied and had little social life. Take the case of Jo, an interior designer from New Jersey.

Jo spent almost every waking minute thinking about her work. She enjoyed work and she certainly was well respected by her colleagues. But the cost for Jo was that her life consisted only of wallpaper and paints, tiles and flooring. She had no social life and felt extremely isolated. When she was not working, she was uptight and depressed about her life in general. On those occasions she would eat—a lot!

If you are like Jo, you achieve a great deal in your work life, but at a high price to yourself. So long as you are busy, however, it is easy to overlook this fact. That is why we call this group "distracters."

2. *Euphoria* A second cause of this driving, striving thinking style relates to the "high" of being successful. We found that for some, the benefit of perfection-seeking came not because such behavior distracted them from negative feelings, but because the striving and success gave them such a deep sense of well-being. The problem with this group was that they were *unable to ease up* on their striving when it came to other areas of their lives. These women got so much out of giving 100 percent that they felt that everything in life had to be done in the same way. Many told us that unless they could do something absolutely right, they would not even want to try. These women had trained themselves to think in an all-or-nothing fashion: either do it perfectly or not at all.

You don't have to be a psychology professor to realize that such thinking imposes a lot of pressure. Since failure was an infrequent experience for these women, they found it even harder to come to terms with it than most. Their expectations of themselves were set so high that when goals were not met, they experienced a great deal of frustration, which led to out-of-control eating. We designated these women "euphorics" since they did seem to genuinely get high on their success. Being happy and proud about your success is a natural response, but it can be counterproductive if you are blurring the distinction between *striving for* success and *having* to achieve it.

Julie is a young account executive in a large advertising agency. Her day consists of nonstop action from the moment she wakes up until the moment she goes to sleep. It's like that seven days a week. She commits herself totally to everything she does, whether she is working, playing tennis, or cooking. That's great, you might think, and it is—until it ceases to be practical. When Julie got frustrated because her tennis game was not as good as she wanted it to be, she took extra lessons to improve. When she did not get instant results, she got even more frustrated and organized yet more coaching. The only problem was that while she was increasing her tennis time, she was also spending more time networking at the office to improve her contacts and feeling guilty about not perfecting a dozen other skills and activities in which she was interested. Ultimately, Julie only could fit so much into her day, and the subsequent lack of progress in her tennis and other social activities was extremely frustrating. She had lost her sense of proportion.

3. Fear of Failure   We also discovered a third group of women whose perfectionism was not occasioned by the euphoria of success. Rather, they were highly motivated by a *fear of failure*. This group was not as well represented as the other types simply because people who are afraid of failure often cope by simply not attempting anything at all. But we found several women who had been in successful careers but whose fear of failure had prevented them from fulfilling their potential.

Take the case of Sally, an experienced personal assistant, who had left her career to raise her children seven years earlier. With the children now in school, the opportunity arose for Sally to take up her career again. The idea of resuming her career was exciting to her, but Sally had serious reservations. She had lost some of her confidence after seven years out of the office routine. Although she could accept rationally that this would return once she eased back into work, she was putting up an emotional block. Analysis of Sally's thoughts revealed that she was having an extremely hard time accepting the fact that she could not *guarantee* that her return to work would be successful. The possibility that she might not be instantly perfect worried her so much that it threw her into a considerable conflict— which resulted in substantial overeating. Fortunately, our Cognitive Change Module helped her identify these thinking errors, and she was able to resume her career successfully.

4. Needing to Be Needed   Albert Ellis, a renowned psychotherapist and founder of Rational-Emotive Therapy, spent many years studying thinking styles. According to Ellis, the most widespread irrational belief is that "one should be loved, or approved of, by everyone." Not only is such a goal unattainable, but striving to be universally popular has distinct disadvantages.

When you're trying to please everyone, the chances are that the one person you are *not* pleasing is yourself. You relegate yourself to a low priority, and this causes considerable stress. When your own needs and wishes take a backseat to the love and approval of others, feelings and even thoughts can be repressed. These repressed feelings eventually manifest themselves as anger, frustration, anxiety, or depression. If you are trying to please people, you can't upset them. You certainly can't say anything unpleasant or critical—even if they're driving you crazy! The quest for approval means that you cannot assert yourself or express your emotions. These repressed feelings build until they need to be released or suppressed with alcohol, drugs, or food. Since it is reasonable to think that the better you do a job the more approval you will get, it is easy to see why perfectionism can stem from this need to be all things to all people.

Crucial Fact #5
You can please all of the people some of the time, and you can please some of the people all the time, but you cannot please all of the people all the time, *nor should you try to do so.*

Trudy works for a well-known banking institution. Her problem is that she finds it nearly impossible to turn down requests that she take on "just one more thing." If extra work has to be done, Trudy is the one who ends up with it. Despite the fact that she is seething with frustration and resentment when her colleagues leave the office at five o'clock sharp while she is still surrounded by a mound of papers, she still finds it difficult to address the issue with her superiors. She rationalizes her position by convincing herself that she is scoring points with her superiors by doing the "right thing." In fact, she is being used.

There's nothing wrong with being popular and accomplished. But the satisfaction of other people should not be the driving force behind your actions, nor should it be the criterion by which you judge your self-worth.

5. Working in a Man's World   All thinking styles are developed as a way of coping with the world at large. There is no question that perfectionistic thinking is developed as a survival tactic in a competitive world. The main problem with thinking styles is that they are developed in childhood in response to a set of family circumstances and situations that do not obtain as we get older. These thinking styles can persist even though they no longer are appropriate. Sometimes, however, entrenched thinking styles *are* adaptive and appropriate. We have seen many women who have used their perfectionism to make an impact in previously male-dominated work environments. The need to be better than male colleagues has been a legitimate concern for women during the workplace revolution of the past two decades. Many have had to prove the legitimacy of their place in business by outperforming their male colleagues. The situation was well summed up by Joanna, who works for a New York brokerage firm: "When I first arrived at this firm, I was the only woman in the office. I felt that if I made one mistake, the men would gloat about it and it might even endanger my chances for advancement in the firm. I was a pioneer in that office and in that profession, and that put a lot of pressure on me. But I was determined to show them that I could do it."

It is not only in the workplace that women face difficult tasks that encourage the thinking styles outlined above. The pressure to fill various roles—career woman, partner, hostess, mother, domestic manager—leads to another problem that underpins the SWEET Syndrome: poor time management. The problems of lifestyle balancing will be addressed in the next chapter.

Can Success Be Harmful to Your Health?

You may be saying to yourself, "What's wrong with being a perfectionist?" You're probably right in believing that your perfectionism has been a factor in your success. But there is something very important you must understand about all personality traits:

Crucial Fact #6
All personality characteristics have the potential to be very positive or very negative, *depending on how they are used.*

You may already have noticed that on some occasions, your character traits are marvelous assets helping you to reach goals and fulfill your potential. On other occasions, those same traits are like millstones around your neck, actually obstructing your progress. You may be like Sue, a Chicago architect, who commented, "My impulsiveness is a mixed blessing. Often it has been a strength, enabling me to be creative and overcome obstacles. On other occasions, it's my worst weakness, sabotaging my plans and getting me into trouble, particularly with my eating."

The secret of success is *not to let your personality traits control you, but for you to understand and harness them.* Look upon these traits as nuclear material that can be either the source of great destruction or the wellspring of incredible energy. We will teach you to understand your characteristics, to identify when they are being used to maximum benefit, and to curb them to limit their destructiveness.

Perfectionism drives your desire for achievement and sparks your motivation. It makes you a skilled worker and a reliable friend, spouse, or parent. It probably is largely responsible for where you are today. But the flip side is that it is also responsible for a tremendous amount of stress and self-imposed pressure. It can make you frustrated and depressed when you don't meet your work and personal goals. It is important for you to know where to draw the line, and in the chapters that follow we will teach you to recognize the difference between *striving for* perfection and *having to be* perfect.

Chapter 5

HOW HIGH A PRIORITY ARE *YOU*?

*I*n the previous chapter we examined how underlying thinking styles give rise to the SWEET Syndrome. These thinking styles also lead to the inefficient use of time. In working with our clients it became evident that many had erratic time-management skills and *often, if not always, put themselves into their hierarchy as their lowest priority*. Their time-management difficulties included:

- Having unrealistic goals

- Being reluctant to delegate

- Being plagued by overcommitment

We found this was true whether our clients were married or unmarried, with or without families, or in or out of a stable relationship. It became apparent to us that food abuse was often the *direct result of erratic time management and lack of lifestyle balance.*

Crucial Fact #7
Your out-of-control eating will stay out of
control until you strike a good balance
with the activities in your life.

Women Who Live Alone

Although many women enjoy the freedom of living
alone, we work with many single women who feel impris-
oned by their own thinking habits, behaviors, and general
lifestyles. While free of husbands, roommates, and children,
many of our unattached clients still were depriving themselves of necessary time and attention. The fact that she does
not have as many pressing domestic commitments as her
married counterparts means that a single woman can devote
even more time, effort, and attention to her work. In many
cases, the extra time that the single person theoretically has
goes into her work and career needs rather than her
personal needs. Sometimes this is the deliberate choice of
the person, but sometimes the extra responsibilities are
thrust on her by colleagues who perceive that a single person
has more time than a married person. Perhaps you can
relate to these comments from Ann, who worked in the
accounting department of a large utility company: "Whenever there is extra work to be done, particularly if it involves
overtime, I'm the one they look to, because they know that

the other women in the department all have family commitments."

There is nothing wrong with working hard, but it is important that you not be taken for granted in your workplace.

What is the result of all this extra involvement in work? Many of our clients in this situation arrived home halfway through the evening, hungry and tired and certainly with no inclination to start preparing food just for themselves. This situation is frequently the setting for out-of-control eating. In fact, it is such a crucial factor that we have developed part of our program, the Lifestyle Balancing Module, specifically to deal with it.

Overinvolvement with work has other unwanted effects for the single person. It can undermine her social life. Long work hours coupled with fatigue are a major barrier to social commitments. Occasionally we have had clients who were using their work load as an excuse for lack of social involvement. More often, however, a poor social life was a habit that had developed from too many late work nights coupled with feelings of inadequacy and self-blame brought about by out-of-control eating. Many women had gotten into the rut of returning home, making poor food choices, and "relaxing" with quick-to-fix, high-calorie foods. The results of this pattern of behavior were often disastrous, as described by one of our clients, a nursing instructor from Illinois: "I started staying late to work on my lectures and seminars. This took up a good deal of time, and I typically finished around seven in the evening. I was tired then and didn't feel like cooking, so I started hitting the fast-food places. Or I would get home and feel too tired to do anything energetic, so I would sit and eat cookies or candy and watch TV or read. Before long I had put on weight, and then I certainly did not want to go out! I became more housebound and put on even more weight. I was disgusted with myself, but as my disgust grew, so did my appetite. It's been awful. I feel so depressed. How can I break this vicious cycle?"

So although the freedom of the single woman may be enviable, the price of that freedom can be loneliness, lack of support, and boredom—all of which are temporarily relieved but ultimately worsened by out-of-control eating.

The single woman with children at home is also in a difficult position. When children are in their teens and old enough to effectively look after themselves, they often act as a source of support. When, however, the children are younger or less responsible, life is extremely demanding for the working mother. Children become the priority, and any free or spare time is spent on their problems. Several of our clients who fell into this category told us that they were rushing constantly between their work and their children. Combine the demands of a career with the rigors of single-handedly raising two children, throw in the perfectionist demand to be all things to all people at work, and you can see why eating problems develop.

Let's consider Judy, who worked in the personnel department of an East Coast bank: Judy had to get up at 6:15 each morning to get herself and her two children, ages eight and six, ready for school. She then set out at 7:15 to drive over an hour to work, where she was kept extremely busy managing the office and support staff. She was good at her job, but because she was so approachable and supportive, she started to become the unofficial company counsellor. People would come to her with personal as well as work problems, and she would listen, support, and advise. At the end of a long day she typically would find herself torn between wanting to leave the office and get home to her children and wanting to lend a sympathetic ear to one of the employees. When she did eventually get home (after another hour on the road), she would be greeted by her children, who wanted her full attention while she tried to prepare the evening meal. She scarcely got time to eat during the day, so by the evening she was definitely suffering from the three H's: hungry, harassed, and hounded. She nibbled food during preparation of the evening meal, and when at last she had some time to herself after the children had gone to bed, she would overindulge with chocolate and cookies. Is it any surprise that Judy had a food problem? Or that her social life was virtually nonexistent? In every area of her life, Judy was giving herself over to serve other people.

Women in a Partnership

Just as children can be a mixed blessing to the single mother, we found that husbands and partners can be a mixed blessing to the women sharing their lives. Husbands can be the source of much comfort, support, and love, but they can also prove to be yet another responsibility. Except in a few very rare cases, women who had working partners were expected not only to work but to take charge of most of the domestic chores as well. Of course there were husbands who did their fair share around the home, but it was usually the working wife who had the prime responsibility for organizing the household, with husbands helping out more as part-time hired hands than supervisors. As a result, the woman was always more involved with household chores even in cases where the work *seemed* to be divided equally between the two partners. Also contributing to this state of affairs might have been the perfectionistic drive of a woman who enjoys challenges, likes to be in control, does not want to be seen as failing in her duties, and would rather do a job herself than delegate it to someone who may only do it adequately. So for our clients, care of husbands and families, although often rewarding, was very time-consuming. One solution to this problem reached by several women was simply to hire staff to do some of the housework and cooking. A creative solution, but one that may not be practical for you.

Many of these women also had a problem when it came to their leisure time. Although the women seemed to have responsibility for domestic chores, husbands and partners often controlled the leisure activities. This can be a satisfactory arrangement as long as both husband and wife have shared interests, or when they both recognize that married couples don't have to do everything together. But all too often, interests are not shared, despite a common misconception that couples have to share everything. We want to stress that you *must use at least part of your spare time to satisfy yourself* rather than always join in activities that hold only marginal interest for you. Simply because your husband likes golf does not mean that *you* have to take it up.

Crucial Fact #8
Everyone needs his or her own time and space and *deserves* to have it.

Consider the case of Virginia, who directed the press department of a Washington, D.C., agency: "My day is very hectic, and I spend a lot of my time meeting people. When I get home, the last thing I want to do is to go out socializing. I just want to sit quietly reading or watching TV. But my husband has a fairly solitary job in which he does not meet people. He is dying to socialize in the evening. To keep the peace, I usually end up going out with him even though I'm tired and would prefer to be at home."

Virginia and her husband are very self-aware people, yet initially they could not see the obvious solution to this problem. It actually came as a surprise to them when we suggested that on some evenings Harry, her husband, could mix with friends on his own while Virginia stayed at home and puttered about.

Virginia and Harry's case is just one example of the importance of learning to deal with anyone—husbands, children, colleagues, and friends—who could, knowingly or otherwise, sabotage your plans. This is such an important issue that we will discuss it in detail in chapters 16 and 17.

Eventually, Virginia was able to address the problem with her husband and they came to an amicable agreement in which their leisure time was suitably divided between joint and individual activities. Accepting the fact that each partner is entitled to his or her own space and time is a crucial first step that is often sufficient to resolve this problem.

Work brought home to be done in the evening and on weekends presents another problem. Often such work is done under the pressure of fatigue at the end of a long day. You may do your work in the den or at a desk which is near the kitchen. Your family may be quiet—children asleep and husband occupied—or they may be snacking while watching TV. It's the perfect time for the SWEET Syndrome to strike. Carbohydrates and high-calorie food are a favorite way of bolstering motivation and concentration. They do this by comforting you and giving you a quick burst of energy. Sometimes it is not you who are working overtime at home, but your partner. In either case, boredom, fatigue, and a sense of deprivation of "fun time" will lead to the frustration that lurks behind out-of-control eating.

Crucial Fact #9
You must have some activities and pastimes that *you* enjoy doing.

A Balanced Lifestyle = A Balanced Diet

It's clear that better use of time can help control the SWEET Syndrome. Your desire for accomplishment at work and at home can erode your precious spare time. A misplaced sense of obligation can have you spending time doing things in which you have little interest. Let's face it: You have enough real obligations in your busy life without adding unnecessarily to the list.

This is why time management is a crucial part of dealing with this syndrome. In Chapter 17, we show how you can set very clear goals to ensure that you allow yourself enough personal time and space. Doing this will allay feelings of being trapped, bored, frustrated, and unfulfilled, and your eating will be brought under control. Our Lifestyle Balancing Module will guide you in achieving this crucial goal.

Chapter 6

DISCOVERING THE *NEW* WILLPOWER

*I*n the preceding chapters we examined some of the causes of the SWEET Syndrome, as well as the factors in daily life that can trigger it. In this chapter, you will come to understand the forces that *keep this behavior going*. It is as important to know what keeps such eating going as it is to understand why it started in the first place, as the Crucial Fact below reveals:

Crucial Fact #10
The events that keep your out-of-control eating going are *not* the same ones that started it in the first place.

We have worked with many women whose overeating began as a response to depression. Yet these women continue to eat excessively long after their depression has lifted. That is why, if you truly want to change your behavior, you must understand what is keeping it going right now, rather than concern yourself too much with past events.

How Habits Develop

The way in which habits develop is fairly simple. A situation gives rise to a particular behavior, in this case, overeating. If the short-term consequences of that eating are good, the chances are increased that the next time you are in that situation, you will repeat the overeating behavior.

Situation (or Cue)	Behavior	Short-term Consequences
Feeling tense	Indulge in high-calorie food	Feel better

Let's take a specific situation: your mid-morning coffee break. The case of Susan, a copywriter for a Midwestern advertising agency, illustrates how such a situation can lead to eating problems. Many of our clients have told us that their unwanted eating habits started when they moved to a new job or were relocated. This is precisely what happened to Susan.

After several years of working in the same office, Susan was relocated to another site following an internal reorganization of the company. At the new location was a vendor who came by at about eleven o'clock each morning selling cookies, sandwiches, pastries, and the like. This was part of the office ritual. The vendor's arrival signalled an unofficial time-out from work. During the first week or so in her new location, Susan was able to resist buying any of the tasty offerings. It was not her practice to eat much at all during the day, let alone sweet things in the middle of the morning. Yet there was increasing pressure on Susan to try some of the Danish pastries (which are one of her favorite indulgences). The mere sight of the food was temptation enough. Besides, many of her colleagues were obviously enjoying these goodies. Susan began to feel left out of things and a little guilty for not joining in! This feeling was fostered in part by others, who were exerting subtle pressure on her to be part of the gang, and partly by herself by being sensitive to this pressure.

One day, during a particularly harassing time at work, Susan decided to indulge. The pastry tasted really good, and Susan remembers thinking that she saw the indulgence as a reward for dealing with a hectic and demanding morning. Although Susan did have some concerns about the effect on her weight, these were far overshadowed when the doughnuts and pastries materialized before her eyes at eleven each morning. Before long she was eating them each day without giving her behavior a second thought. Not only did Susan (and her colleagues) look forward to the arrival of the cakes, but they actually started to feel hungry *before* the food arrived. Susan noticed that about five minutes before the vendor showed up, she could feel herself salivating and hear her stomach growling! After a few months of this, Susan decided that she really ought to stop this habit, but no matter how hard she tried to convince herself of the negative effects of these indulgences, the pastries seemed magnetically to pull her towards them. The *more* she tried to stop, the *more difficult* it became.

Crucial Fact #11
Your behavior is controlled much more by short-term, positive effects than by long-term, negative ones. The immediate satisfaction of eating your favorite foods outweighs the long-term penalty of weight gain.

Why You Have No Control Over Food When You Do Over Everything Else

Have you experienced the frustrating feeling of being unable to control your eating? All of the participants in our weight education program, whether or not they suffer from the SWEET Syndrome, report that there are certain foods over which they feel they have little control. As soon as they come into contact with these foods, they feel that *it is inevitable* that they will eat them. As one woman so succinctly put it, "I feel as if the food controls me, not the other way around." We have found that this feeling usually occurs in response to certain *trigger events* at work or at home.

The Trigger Event Profile

In order to identify the trigger events in your life that result in overeating and the positive short-term consequences that reinforce the habit, spend a few minutes completing the exercise below on a separate sheet of paper. Be as specific as possible when describing the trigger events. For example, your excessive eating may occur in the middle of the afternoon, but it may be most acute when there is no one else around, or perhaps when you have had a light lunch and are working under pressure. Being as specific as possible will help you isolate the key elements of the situation that prompt your craving. Be specific when describing the foods you typically eat in these situations. Describe the type and amount of food you usually eat. Most people have about three situations that are really problematic, but in this exercise describe *any* situation that is potentially troublesome and leads to craving.

Here's how Susan completed her exercise.

Trigger Events	Foods	Short-term Consequence	Long-term Consequence
Office coffee break	Pastry (1 or 2)	Energy boost	Guilt Weight gain Frustration

Perhaps this exercise has highlighted your feeling of helplessness about certain foods and situations. You may also feel that *once you've started eating these foods, you can't stop until they're all gone!* Like Susan, you may have noticed that the harder you try to stop, the more difficult it seems to be. For the woman who is used to being in command of herself, this lack of control is extremely unsettling. It becomes a vicious cycle: the more unsuccessful at control you are, the more frustrated you get, and the more you want to eat!

It's easy to become angry at yourself for having no willpower and self-control. That's where our program comes into its own. We will teach you the skills that will enable you to practice discipline and self-control, without self-abuse.

Crucial Fact #12
Willpower is not something you are born with or without. It involves *skills* that can be *learned.*

But why should people who normally can do whatever they put their minds to experience such frustration when it comes to controlling what they eat?

The Biochemical Connection

The reason you can't change your out-of-control eating by simply putting your mind to it is that *change involves more than your mind*—it involves your body as well, and that's where the main problem lies.

Each time you consume those goodies, you are training your body. Take the eating in the office example we used above. Each time Susan eats in the office like this, she is teaching her body to *expect food whenever she is in that*

68

situation. That's why the salivating and stomach growling start *before* the pastries arrive.

You probably are familiar with the classic experiment conducted by the Russian physiologist Ivan Pavlov at the beginning of the century. He demonstrated that by initially pairing a tone with food, he could eventually get dogs to anticipate food merely by presenting the tone. Within a relatively short space of time the animals salivated at the sound of the tone even when no food was present. This simple experiment demonstrates the power of association and the ease with which our bodies can be trained.

Since Pavlov, there have been many studies that demonstrate how important environmental cues are in triggering our behavior. A series of studies conducted in New York by Professor Stanley Schachter in the late 1960s and replicated many times since showed that eating was set off by environmental cues rather than hunger. In one experiment the clocks were turned forward, making subjects think it was noon when it was really eleven o'clock. Subjects ate more because they thought it was lunch time!

In another study the mere sight of food brought about an increase in insulin flow. Insulin, which regulates your blood-sugar level, is released when you eat sweet or starchy foods. If insulin is released before you eat, it will lower your blood-sugar level to a point that will produce real sensations of hunger. So you can see that once you have trained your body to expect food, it will produce biochemical changes that will make it very difficult for you to resist eating.

Fortunately, we train our bodies to respond to very *specific situations.* Susan, for example, did not feel hungry and start to salivate every day at eleven o'clock. She did this *only* when it was eleven in the morning on a weekday at the office. She did not give food a passing thought at the same time at home during weekends or even during the week in a different location.

> **Crucial Fact #13**
> **The conditioning of our bodies is very situation-specific.**

That our conditioning is so specific accounts for the fact that it is so much easier to stop smoking or change eating habits when you are away from your normal environment. A new environment provides fewer cues that trigger the conditioned behavior than your usual setting does. That's why many of our clients who struggle against cravings every day of their lives at home have virtually no problems at all when they come to South Carolina to participate in the Hilton Head Program. The usual cues that trigger these cravings simply are not there.

Some remarkable animal experiments have demonstrated how much biology is controlled by very specific environmental cues. A Canadian experiment conducted in the 1970s showed that when drug-addicted laboratory rats were taken off heroin and remained in their *usual* cages, they demonstrated the expected, typical withdrawal symptoms. When, however, the rats were withdrawn from heroin and placed in *new* cages that had no association with drugs, they demonstrated virtually no withdrawal whatsoever! Simply changing the cages was enough to virtually wipe out the strong effect of heroin withdrawal. Strong associations to very specific situations can turn our biology on and off without our realizing what is happening.

Once you have built up a habit of eating in a particular situation, your body simply begins to expect food. It will release insulin in anticipation of food; it will produce salivary flow; it will initiate gastric contractions. Your body will respond this way in any situation in which you typically eat *and* whenever you start to eat foods that you eat a lot of.

Crucial Fact #14
Your *physiological* response to food and eating situations is a crucial reason why you find it so difficult to control your eating.

Close your eyes and think of your favorite food. Imagine it very vividly. See if you can't smell it or even taste it. Focus on the food for about thirty seconds. Try it now.

Perhaps you are now feeling a little hungry. Perhaps you are salivating a little. Your jaw muscles might be a bit tight.

You might well be feeling anxious. These are responses brought about merely by *thinking* about food! You see how well you've trained that body of yours!

The New Willpower Explained

Perhaps now you realize why on hundreds of occasions you have promised yourself "just one small bite," and on hundreds of occasions you have ended up taking lots of large ones. But don't despair. It *is* possible to learn to have one small bite and stop, and it *is* possible to learn to refuse your favorite food. The secret of possessing such unlikely willpower lies in retraining your body and *breaking the biochemical links* between your body and the trigger events that cause you to eat.

Merely exhorting yourself to have more willpower will not work. Willpower can be effective only if you have control over these conditioned bodily responses. By gaining control of your body's responses, it is possible to implement a *new willpower* that will enable you to exercise control over food craving and eating situations.

Why Avoidance Strategies Don't Work

Many sources of help for out-of-control eaters suggest that the way to deal with the problem is simply to avoid situations in which food seems so tempting that you are lured beyond your control. This may seem like sensible advice if the triggers for your overeating are exotic Christmas cakes, royal tea parties, and other special occasions. You can avoid many of those things most of the time without major disruption to your life. But if the triggers to your eating happen to be tiredness, tension, boredom, or even just four o'clock in the afternoon, you're in trouble, because these things cannot be easily avoided. Even if you *could* avoid some of these triggers to your overeating, how helpful would it be?

Let's construct a fudge shop scenario. (It could be the ice-cream parlor, or the doughnut shop, or any place that triggers your desire to eat.) Each time you pass the fudge shop your attention is caught. You find yourself looking in the window, and the sight of your favorite fudge sets off a physiological response. Your body is gearing up to eat. It *expects* you to have some fudge. Despite your best intentions, you find yourself inside the shop. There you are confronted with the smell of the goodies. The assistant offers you a free taste. You are now being *bombarded with cues to eat* and your body has reached the *foregone conclusion* that you are going to eat. You are salivating and your stomach even begins to growl! You make some excuse to yourself about getting some fudge for your friend's niece who might be coming into town in two weeks' time, and you buy some of your favorite fudge. You decide to take a little taste to make sure that the fudge really is okay, so you eat one square. Now your body really gets into high gear as it prepares to get yet more. Despite your best intentions, you find yourself eating four more squares, after which you give up the pretense and eat the rest. For a few microseconds you bask in the pleasure of satisfying your need, but before long guilt sets in. You feel guilty and extremely angry with yourself. You promise yourself that you are never going to eat another piece of fudge. You also decide that you are going to eat nothing more that day both to punish yourself and to minimize the weight gain.

Now, suppose you do manage to avoid fudge and the fudge shop for the next two years. What happens?

Both our research and that of other experts around the world suggest that this type of avoidance strategy does not work in the long run. For a start, avoiding the fudge shop is an admission that you have no control over your desires. You are operating under the conviction that fudge is your downfall, and you are waiting for the inevitable to happen. So what happens when after two years you come face to face with fudge again? Have all those physical responses to the sight, smell, and taste of fudge disappeared? Of course not. In fact, they are likely to be as strong as ever. Your two-year avoidance of fudge has done nothing to change your powerful and irresistible physiological response to it. As soon as you go back into that fudge shop, you are very literally back to square one.

Crucial Fact #15
Avoidance strategies are useful in the short term but do nothing to change the underlying problems.

If avoidance is not a useful strategy, what is? By now it should be clear to you that the way to conquer this problem is to change your underlying physiological response to your favorite foods and trigger situations. *Until you do this you will have only temporary solutions at best.* Our craving-control techniques will enable you to change your physical responses so that it is *you that controls the food, not the other way around.* By exposing themselves to problematic situations in a gradual way, and by using a special pattern of eating, our clients have changed their biochemical responses to foods and have gained control of their eating.

When we started our craving control program at the Hilton Head Health Institute after several years of research, we knew that we had found an effective technique. Our clients were enthusiastic not only about the results, but also about how *quickly* they had progressed. Let's use the case of Kelly as an example.

Kelly was a computer systems analyst who suffered from the SWEET Syndrome. Her weakness was ice cream. She was resigned to the fact that this food controlled her and that she must avoid it at all costs. But no matter how hard she tried, she would always end up eating it—lots of it. She was angry at herself, depressed, and about 20 pounds overweight.

Using the same craving control program that is described later in this book, Kelly gradually confronted her ice-cream habit by at first going briefly into ice-cream parlors and shops selling ice cream. As her confidence increased, she put herself in more and more challenging situations for longer periods of time, each time successfully avoiding eating. The difficulty of the situation varied according to Kelly's degree of hunger and stress. After three weeks and about eight sessions, she told us: "I really feel as if I'm getting control. I have confidence that I can resist the ice cream, so I no longer need to avoid the places where I can find it. What is really amazing is that it took me ten years to build this habit and just a few sessions to break it!"

> **Crucial Fact #16**
> With the right techniques, you can retrain your body's response to food very quickly, and can reverse habits of many years' standing in just a few sessions.

Most of our clients claim that this craving control technique actually reduces the *intensity* of their desire for their favorite foods, as well as strengthening their ability to resist them. Karen, a model who loved cookies, told us: "What amazed me was that after a while cookies really did not seem to be all that attractive to me. I can take them or leave them."

This technique does not change your basic food preferences and tendencies. If you are someone who has a "sweet tooth," you'll still have a sweet tooth after using this method. But you will be far less anxious when you are exposed to these foods because you will not feel as if you are fighting a losing battle against the inevitable. As a result, the foods will seem less attractive and tempting to you and you will be able to take them or leave them. The power of choice will rest with you!

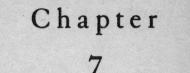

Chapter 7

PREPARING
YOURSELF
MENTALLY

*Accepting the Three Truths
of Life*

*A*lthough this program is straightforward and easy to follow, it requires a commitment from you. It is essential to examine three truths of life and work to program them into your mind. If you consider these truths each and every day, you will be successful at developing a more balanced, more rewarding life.

The three truths of life are:

Truth #1. Change is an essential part of life.

Truth #2. Restraint and self-management are necessary for personal growth.

Truth #3. Personal difficulties and challenges are what life is all about.

Let's examine these truths one at a time and look at them more closely.

Accepting Change as Inevitable

You might be thinking, "Of course I'm ready and willing to change. Out-of-control eating is making my life miserable. It makes me less productive as well. Why wouldn't I want to change?" Believe it or not, there may be a part of you, albeit a small part, that doesn't want anything to do with change.

Change is often difficult to accept, even though it may be for the best. Even the most psychologically miserable person may, at some level, resist change. Change is difficult to accept both consciously and unconsciously because it is a kind of stress on the mind and body. Even if you are very committed to change, and even if you strongly believe that change is necessary, there still will be a part of you that says, "NO!" Or at least, "Wait a minute. Let's move slowly because I'm not sure what these changes will bring." You often are not even aware of these mental blocks because they are usually embedded deep in your mind.

Our bodies and minds have a natural urge to maintain the status quo. Physiologists use the term *homeostasis* to describe this tendency of the body to maintain a balance among internal bodily conditions. The mind and body are constantly working to keep conditions within normal limits. It is, in most cases, a mechanism that insures our survival amid the thousands of fluctuating situations we face each day. One example of homeostasis is the body's mechanism for maintaining a temperature of 98.6° F. by inducing sweating to cool the body when your temperature goes up and shivering to heat the body when you are too cold.

Mental homeostasis is not as easy to understand. Unlike body temperature, what is normal for mental homeostasis varies from one person to another. Research shows that *your mind accepts as normal any behavior that is habitual.* So, as you develop habits (both good and bad ones) throughout your life, your mind accepts them as being the normal standard. Once that acceptance has occurred, your mind and body will resist any change in the system because change is viewed as a threat to mental and physical stability and well-being. The body will act in the same protective way whether your temperature increases dramatically due to fever, or whether your negative eating habits are changing as a result of a treatment program.

It's important to understand that change is not impossible because of this tendency to maintain homeostasis. But you should know that you may experience some internal resistance to change that may seem to slow your progress or confuse you. Just remember that such resistance is normal and that, with the proper attitude, you can overcome that resistance.

Another important reason why you may feel internal resistance to change is that habits *serve a purpose.* They provide you with a way to cope with stress in your life and give you a sense of release from the many responsibilities and controls that are part of a busy person's life. Part of you is actually afraid to give up this coping mechanism—even though it is an unhealthy one—for fear that no better alternative will be available. To your unconscious mind, *some* means of coping is better than no way to cope at all.

This is why the Hilton Head Program teaches you to

condition your mind and body very gradually. By the time you give up your old eating habits, you will be well on your way to learning new, more adaptive ways to deal with the stress in your life.

The important thing for you to remember is that even though your body resists change, change is not only inevitable, but it is an *absolute necessity* of life.

The following Crucial Fact, borrowed from the distinguished 19th-century Catholic scholar John Cardinal Newman, is a thought to remember always:

Crucial Fact #17
"To live is to change, and to be perfect is to change often."

Life is like a clear mountain stream that draws its sustenance from its flowing motion. If that flow were to stop, the water would stagnate and the living things in the water would die. If you were to stop changing, you, too, would stagnate emotionally and physically.

Learn to welcome change and accept it. Seeking out change every day of your life affirms your commitment to being alive. Change is positive and healthy. Most important of all, view change as a definite possibility in your own life. You will change more quickly if you open your mind to it and realize that although new habits may feel a bit uncomfortable at first, they will become old friends before you know it.

Why Giving Up Some Pleasure Is Good for You

The words *self-discipline* and *self-restraint* often bring mixed feelings. Many people say that they want or need to be more self-disciplined, but when it comes right down to it, they view restraint and delay of gratification in very negative terms. A 34-year-old senior vice-president of a large textile manufacturing company once said to us, "A life of total willpower sounds dull to me. That would take away my spontaneity and turn me into a robot, programmed to make perfect responses all the time."

Actually, this is far from the goal we would set for you. Since control is posing a problem for you that is reflected in your eating habits—too much control at times and too little at others—we certainly do not want to make you more controlled. What we are after is *flexibility*. You should be able to choose to discipline yourself when you need to. Right now you may feel that in your busy work and home life, you have to be controlled just to keep up. The key word in this discussion is *choice*. Self-discipline and restraint should be seen as positive choices you are making, rather than as ways of responding that are forced upon you.

One further point deserves mention. Don't confuse being organized with being controlled. You might be asking yourself, "How can I let go of control without creating chaos in my life?" The goal is certainly not to produce disorder. Using this program, you will continue to be organized and productive, but in a more flexible, less driven way. The key is finding a healthy balance.

> **Crucial Fact #18**
> Viewing self-management as both a
> personal choice and a necessary ingredient
> of life is essential to conquering the
> SWEET Syndrome.

The power of choice and the power to manage your own life are essential for personal growth and change. We prefer to use the term *self-management* rather than will-power, self-discipline, or self-control to describe the power of choice. This term implies that the discipline lies within *you*.

When you think in terms of self-management, you are no longer restraining your desire for ice cream (to take one example) because you *have* to, but because you *want* to. This doesn't mean that this restraint will be easy or that you don't sometimes resent making the choice to forego the ice cream. It does not mean, in other words, that you are *denying* that you feel the way you do. Denial of feelings comes from a wish to be perfect—and we know that the pressure to be perfect can lead to precisely the kind of eating that you want to get away from.

Much of what we are talking about has to do with growing up. A large part of maturity and individual free-dom is related to the extent to which you are willing to give up old satisfactions. Throughout our lives we are continually giving up things in order to grow. We give up dependence on parents so we can become independent adults, just as we give up our mother's breast so we can drink from a glass on our own.

Restraining our desires is a form of letting go of the past. Otherwise, we would remain infantile and dependent the rest of our lives. As you know, there are many "adults" who are grown-up babies, complaining throughout life, refusing to give up anything that they enjoy no matter what the consequences to them or anyone else.

By giving up your out-of-control eating, even though you realize that the foods give you pleasure, you are proclaiming your individuality and personal freedom. You are growing emotionally and mentally. You are declaring war on behavior that has been holding you back for too long. Most importantly, you are showing yourself that you are capable of giving up a part of you that you simply don't need anymore.

Since life is a series of self-management decisions such as this one, you are also building a sense of mastery and confidence that you will draw upon the next time you need to give something up in order to grow. That time will come—and come often. But rather than feel resentful, you will realize that life and personal growth require restraint and, at times, giving up some of the things that we love and that make us feel comfortable and safe.

Why You Shouldn't Pave the Road of Life

The road of life is bumpy. Life is never as smooth as we would like it to be. Let's suppose that we could magically make all your difficulties disappear so that your life would be smooth, steady, and worry-free forever. Would you then have found heaven on earth? Would you then be perfectly happy? Definitely not! In fact, because you are an intelligent, sophisticated, and complex personality, we would predict that you would be more miserable than before.

Brenda is a prime example of this fact. Several years ago, Brenda started a small commercial real estate business in Chicago. She was young, energetic, and determined to succeed. By the time she was 30, Brenda's firm had grown into a multi-million-dollar operation. However, with success came frustration and aggravation with the day-to-day problems that crop up in a high-powered real estate business. As the business grew, Brenda developed a periodic out-of-control eating problem. In both her business dealings and in her eating she evidenced all-or-nothing control, going from one extreme to another. On some days she paced herself, delegated tasks to others, and took time out for meals and aerobic dance classes. More often than not, however, Brenda would push herself to the limit, seeing clients for 15 hours a day, eating junk food on the run, and skipping her scheduled exercise class.

Finally, on one of her most hectic business days when nothing was going right, Brenda decided that she'd had enough. She determined that the solution to her problems was to smooth out her life by selling the business. She put it up for sale and within six months had found a buyer who offered her an impressive price, which she accepted. All of a sudden, Brenda was free of her problems.

Brenda now had no worries, no stress. She invested her money and was financially set for the rest of her life. For the next several months she traveled to all of the exotic places she had always dreamed about—Bali, the Orient, Tahiti, and Australia. As time went by, however, she began to feel bored and depressed. Her out-of-control eating episodes *increased* in frequency. She was feeling more and more miserable.

When Brenda first consulted us about her eating problem, she learned that, like most people, she *needed* problems and stresses in order to verify her existence in the world. Some women—smart, self-demanding women—need the challenge of problems more than most. They are powerful, take-charge people who must meet and surmount difficulties in order to feel fulfilled in their lives.

> **Crucial Fact #19**
> Once you accept that life is sometimes difficult and always will be that way, you are well on your way to conquering the SWEET Syndrome.

The very essence of life is change and challenge, coupled with our attempts to cope, overcome, and conquer in the face of adversity. Once you accept this basic truth, your life and your problems will actually seem *easier* to deal with. You will accept difficulties as the norm. You will accept challenge as life itself.

People who do not accept the fact that life is difficult often find themselves living in the future. They get into the habit of thinking, "Once this problem is over, everything will be okay again," or "Maybe next year will be a better one and I'll finally be happy," or "Next time I'll hit on the right solution, and then my life will go smoothly." This type of thinking leads you to miss out on the joys of daily living.

Life is a journey, a grand excursion that is meant to be experienced mile by mile. Too many people think about the destination, and completely miss the excitement of the trip itself.

So, before you read further, spend a few minutes preparing your mind by doing a little in-depth self-analysis. Answer the following questions honestly and think about your responses in relation to what we have discussed in this chapter.

The Life Challenge Quiz

Question 1: What are some of the ways in which you try to make your life run smoothly and without change, both at work and at home?

> *Some Considerations:* In answering this question, consider even seemingly insignificant ways in which you keep your life the same. For example, do you follow a standard routine in the morning for getting up and getting ready for work? Do you try to standardize the routines of your family members? Is everything on your desk at work "just so"? Do you go through an established ritual just after you arrive at work each day

or right before you leave in the evening? Don't find fault with yourself over your routines; simply identify them and think about them. After you list the ways in which you keep your life the same, think about *why* you do those things the way you do. Why are certain routines so important to you?

Question 2: How do you react to sudden changes in your life?

Some Considerations: Think about all changes, from trivial to crucial ones. Do you view these changes as threats rather than as interesting challenges? What changes have occurred in your life in the past 30 days and how did you react to them? Did you move; were you assigned new responsibilities at work; did you have a falling-out with a friend? How could you have changed your attitude toward those changes to make them more positive experiences?

Question 3: Do you have a need to "put things in order" or "take care of things" when events are not as they should be at work or at home?

Some Considerations: Are you always the one who is adjusting a crooked picture on the wall or trying to patch up a disagreement between family members or co-workers? If so, this may reflect your need to maintain homeostasis in life—to avoid change. As you will see as you progress through the Hilton Head Program, change is a positive factor in living. It may scare you at first, because it goes against your natural tendency to keep everything in a certain order. After a while, however, you will welcome change and realize the very positive influence it can have on your life.

Question 4: Do you resent even small problems in your life?

Some Considerations: Consider all the problems you have encountered lately—big and small ones. When such difficulties come into your life, do you resent them or ask, "Why me?" Remember, adversity and self-management are realities of life. They are not only inevitable but *essential* to your full and complete growth as a person. From successfully navigating the rocky road of life comes much of our joy in living.

Chapter
8

PREPARING
YOUR
SCHEDULE

*T*his program requires *active* participation from you. We will be asking you to put specific deconditioning routines into practice for 12 days, one hour per day. Think of these routines as strategies to be completed before going to the next chapter.

> **Crucial Fact #20**
> For the Hilton Head Program to be maximally effective, you must become an active participant in following it.

It is also important to follow the program to the letter with no deviations. If you omit part of the treatment program because you feel it does not apply in your case, you will not receive its maximum benefit. Have faith that this program will work for you just as it has worked for many other women. Undergoing the *complete* program is essential for *lasting* change.

> **Crucial Fact #21**
> To get the results you want, you must
> follow the Hilton Head Program exactly
> as it is outlined, making no changes in
> format or sequence.

Plan to spend approximately one hour each day for the next 12 days carrying out the program's techniques. We say "approximately" because your rate of progress depends on your own unique lifestyle, and lifestyles vary slightly from person to person. Take sufficient time to successfully complete one strategy before going on to the next one. In 12 days you will be able to learn the basics of the program, which you will then put into practice in your daily life.

First, read through the program described in the following chapters. Then block off the necessary treatment times in your schedule. Finally, go through the treatment chapters one at a time, putting each step of the program into practice.

The program is easy to follow and will not be disruptive to your schedule. Therefore, *do not delay* implementing the program until you can find the "right" time, when there are fewer distractions in your work, family, or social schedules. Your life is always going to be busy, and this program is designed to help you deal with exactly this fact. The time to begin is now! Otherwise, you will have to live with out-of-control eating that much longer.

The only exception to this rule would be if you are planning a vacation or an extensive business trip over the next two weeks. In that case, wait until you are back into your routine. However, if travel is an integral part of your life, then get started right away. If you wait, you'll be missing out on the freedom from food that you deserve.

Twelve Days to a New Life

Over the next two weeks you will be changing your body, your mind, and even your life. Our goals and yours will be to provide you with:

- Freedom *forever* from out-of-control eating

- A new way of thinking that will enable you to turn career and personal stress into positive energy

- A more balanced approach to life that will prove beneficial both to your career goals and your personal happiness

To accomplish these goals we will be concentrating on three major areas, or *modules,* each designed to combat a specific element of the SWEET Syndrome. These three treatment modules are:

- The Cognitive Change Module

- The Craving Control Ladder Module

- The Lifestyle Balancing Module

These modules will be explained in detail in the following chapters with step-by-step instructions on how to put one into practice.

The 12 days of the program will be divided as follows:

- Cognitive Change Module: 4 days

- Craving Control Ladder Module: 5 days

- Lifestyle Balancing Module: 3 days

Creating Your Treatment Notebook

Throughout the treatment modules we will be referring to a *treatment notebook*. Any spiral or looseleaf notebook will serve the purpose. Make sure you purchase one before you begin, because your notebook will be very important in helping you complete the techniques we describe.

The Case of Audrey   To give you a better idea of how the program works, let us tell you about Audrey, a 27-year-old bond broker working for a major brokerage firm on Wall Street. Audrey lives life in the fast lane and is advancing in the financial world at an impressive pace. Audrey has chosen to remain single and, since she has no family obligations, often works late at the office on weekdays and brings work home with her on weekends.

Audrey has always been interested in fitness and nutrition, primarily to keep herself feeling and looking good. She prides herself on having a sleek, professional appearance. Besides, with the intensity of her work in the bond market, she needs all the stamina she can muster.

About three years prior to consulting us, she began to experience periodic episodes of out-of-control eating. These episodes seemed innocent enough at first: a pint of chocolate ice cream one evening and, a couple of weeks later, six chocolate-covered doughnuts on a Sunday afternoon.

As time went on, these episodes began to occur about twice a week. Audrey now found that in order to keep to her ideal weight of 120 pounds, she had to watch her calorie intake and exercise even more than normal to make up for these periodic overindulgences. Even a three- or four-pound weight gain made her feel bloated and sluggish. She felt that such feelings had a definite negative infuence on her mental sharpness at work. In her highly competitive career, where mistakes in judgment and timing could be devastating, such difficulties would not be tolerated for long. More importantly, Audrey would not tolerate such behavior in herself for long.

One day one of our clients told Audrey about our treatment program at the Hilton Head Health Institute. Audrey called us the same day and within a week was on a plane headed to South Carolina.

Over a 12-day period we worked with Audrey and taught her the secrets of the Hilton Head plan. She learned our techniques for balancing the control in her life, so that she was neither overly controlled nor undercontrolled. It was as if she came to us with two distinct personalities—one very much in control and the other totally out of control—and ended up with only one, which was a balance of both.

Audrey's perfectionistic thinking patterns were modified by means of our Cognitive Change Module. We helped

Audrey analyze her thinking patterns (a technique you will be learning to accomplish on your own) and then assisted her in recording audiotapes of new, less constrictive thought patterns. Through repeated practice with these tapes, she began to reprogram her mind. We concentrated especially on thoughts and feelings that in the past had triggered out-of-control eating.

Then we put Audrey through our Craving Control Ladder Module. Using this module, her body was deconditioned and desensitized to the thought and sight of foods that were high on her craving list. This phase of treatment required her actually to look at, touch, and even taste foods that she associated with out-of-control eating. In the beginning such exposures to food occurred under "neutral" emotional conditions. As treatment progressed, she was exposed to these foods while she was tired or while under stresses similar to those that normally triggered her eating. During this deconditioning process Audrey gained more and more mastery over food.

Finally, by following the Lifestyle Balancing Module, Audrey increased her sense of personal freedom while maintaining a busy, competitive career. Audrey now has a balanced life in which she is able to structure her career but also keep enough time for herself.

She is in control of her eating and is pursuing a busy career and social life without the self-demanding, self-defeating thoughts and behaviors that had led to the SWEET Syndrome.

Now it's your turn to claim that freedom!

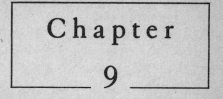

Chapter 9

THE COGNITIVE
CHANGE MODULE:
DAY 1

*Getting Your Thoughts
Out of Your Head*

*T*he first step in the Hilton Head Program involves a change in you that is relatively simple to execute but profound in its results. The Cognitive Change Module will teach you how to change the way you think, particularly the way you think about yourself, your work, your body, and your eating.

But aren't thoughts automatic, much like breathing and heart rate? Can you change an experience that occurs so naturally and fortuitously? Certainly you can.

Our Cognitive Change Module is designed to create actual changes in your way of thinking. Simply paying attention to the thoughts that trigger out-of-control eating is not enough. In fact, *awareness without change will make matters worse* because you will worry about why you are not able to change the unhealthy thoughts in your mind.

Thinking is nothing more than *subvocal speech*. This term literally means talking to yourself with words that cannot be heard by anyone else. Just as you can learn to speak differently, you can also learn to think differently. As you will see, as soon as you can get your thoughts out of your head and can analyze them, they will be easily controlled.

The trouble with thoughts, particularly the thoughts that cause the SWEET Syndrome, is that they constitute a very one-sided conversation. You hear them in your head but you rarely talk back, question, or challenge them. You bow to the powerful voice of the "master" of your mind.

It's time to change all that. We are going to help you see that *you* are the master. Using the Cognitive Change Module, you will learn how to identify the types of thoughts that contribute most to out-of-control eating, erase those thoughts from your mind, and replace your old thinking style with positive, productive self-talk.

Interrupting Your Mental Monologue

To implement the Cognitive Change Module, you will need an audio tape recorder and a blank tape. You also will need to be certain that the recorder has either a built-in microphone or a microphone attachment that you can plug into it. Next, you will need a pen or pencil and the treatment notebook we spoke about earlier.

Be prepared to examine your thoughts in an honest and forthright manner. But be patient with yourself, too—don't expect your thoughts to change overnight. Putting new thoughts in your mind is a lot like a surgeon implanting a new kidney in your body. Just as your body may at first reject this transplanted organ, so, too, your mind may instinctively try to reject a new thought because it is strange and foreign.

Deborah is a 32-year-old editor for a well-respected fashion magazine. When she first consulted us about her periodic out-of-control eating, we determined that she had been suffering from the SWEET Syndrome for about three years. Deborah took pride in her appearance. Most of the time she counted calories, ate nutritious foods, and exercised regularly. On an increasingly frequent basis, however, she reacted to the immense work load and deadlines at the magazine with periodic bingeing (primarily foods high in sugar, such as candy, ice cream, and cookies). These out-of-control eating episodes were combined with a complete discontinuation of her exercise routine and usually lasted about three or four days.

Although Deborah was extremely successful in using our program, she did experience psychological resistance during the Cognitive Change Module phase. This resistance was especially obvious when she was trying to change her pattern of all-or-nothing perfectionistic thinking. During one instance, Deborah was in her office working on an editorial assignment that was due in two days. It was 6:30 P.M. and she had about two more hours of work to complete the project. She had also promised two friends that she would meet them for a drink and dinner at 7:00 P.M.

Her thoughts at the time were, "Even though I've been working all day on this article and it's late, I *must* finish what I started. I'll just have to cancel the dinner with Sara and Michelle." This inflexible thinking caused Deborah to stay at work that night until nine o'clock. She went home feeling overly tired, depressed, and put-upon, and proceeded to eat a large bag of cookies.

We worked with Deborah to help her practice new, more flexible thought patterns. For example, she repeatedly practiced thinking, "Relax! I've been working on this assignment all day. I deserve a break. I know I can finish early in the morning, so there's no need to stay late tonight. I'm being too hard on myself. I must learn to balance my life."

As Deborah practiced this new way of thinking, the enemy within began to rear its ugly head. Something in her resisted these new, healthier ways of thinking. As she practiced, her mind wandered to such thoughts as "This is not really how I think. This is unnatural," or "This is silly. I'll never be able to change my thoughts. I've been thinking the same way for years and it's too late to change now."

While this resistance slowed her progress a bit, Deborah overcame her own protests by seeing them for what they really were: namely, mere *defense mechanisms designed to maintain the status quo.* By not listening to the content of these words of resistance, she began to get the new, healthier message. Once she refused to pay attention to the enemy within, her progress improved dramatically.

You can learn a valuable lesson from Deborah. Resistance will occur, but your best defense is simply to *recognize it for what it is, and ignore it.* Soon, these intrusive thoughts will disappear altogether. This will pave the way for a complete reprogramming of your mind and an end to your eating problems.

Four Days to Flexibility Thinking

Now you are ready to begin the first four days of the 12-day program. This chapter will give you instructions to follow for Day 1.

During this time you will be learning how to rid yourself of old ways of thinking, and how to replace them with what we call *flexibility thinking*. Flexibility thinking puts you in charge of the mental monologue that is having so much influence over your behavior. It enables you to debate issues with yourself, to challenge and change thinking mistakes you have been making all your life.

It is important to view your thinking simply as mistaken or erroneous thinking rather than as a psychological problem or negative personality trait. With a little effort we can all profit from our mistakes. In this age of psychological enlightenment, it is tempting to complicate problems by designing elaborate theories to explain our actions. We have found that a direct learning method is the quickest and most effective way of changing thought patterns—even ones that have been influencing you all of your life.

Listening to the Voice Within

Before you can change your thinking patterns you must first find out what they are. Now is the time you will need the tape recorder, notebook, and pen that we discussed previously. On this first day of the Hilton Head Program, *think about three separate issues in your life and, as you think about them, record your thoughts into the tape recorder.*

> **Crucial Fact #22**
> Before you can change your way of thinking you must get your thoughts out of your head by recording them into a tape recorder or writing them down.

As you do this, don't try to analyze your thinking or consider what it means. Just say your thoughts aloud into the recorder. Do not edit or organize your thoughts as they come to your mind. Don't try to put them in other words. Don't try to make sense out of them. Just speak them as they come into your head, even if some of the thoughts are simply words or phrases.

If you do not own a tape recorder, write your thoughts in your notebook. However, we suggest that you borrow or purchase a tape recorder for this exercise. Actually speaking your thoughts enables you to be more spontaneous and accurate. Moreover, Days 3 and 4, during which you learn to change your thinking habits, progress much faster if you have a tape recorder.

Here is what Deborah (in the case mentioned previously) recorded when she put this exercise into practice immediately after an episode of out-of-control eating:

Oh, no! I've done it again! This is terrible! Why can't I control my cravings? Why can't I have more self-discipline? Why can't I be like other people? Damn! This makes me so mad! What would people think of me if they knew about this? I know they would think of me as an undisciplined person who should not be trusted with important assignments. I'm being irresponsible and uncontrolled. I hate myself when this happens. I have no willpower. I'm totally out of control now and I'll probably keep eating like this all weekend. What difference does it make anyway? My life is a disaster.

Now it's your turn. Think about one of your out-of-control eating episodes. If you've had one recently, perhaps in the last few days or perhaps even now, so much the better. Put yourself back in that situation mentally and emotionally. Try to relive the experience and the feelings, moment by moment. Now tune into your thinking process. As the thoughts surface, record them on your tape. Remember to *speak them exactly as they come to your mind* without analyzing them.

To help yourself along in this exercise, complete the following sentences:

- Whenever I think about my uncontrolled eating it makes me feel so . . .

- The main thing that upsets me about my eating is . . .

- If I continue to eat like this, then . . .

- The fact that I cannot control my eating indicates that I am . . .

- If other people knew about my eating, they would think . . .

- Once I get started with my uncontrolled eating, I will . . .

Expanding the Use of This Technique

After you have completed this task, go on to another stressful situation in your life. Try the same procedure using a problem in your career such as a disagreement with your boss or a co-worker, or how you deal with an overloaded, hectic schedule. Use a situation that is fresh in your mind, perhaps something that happened today.

Finally, use the same procedure to monitor your thoughts about a situation involving your personal relationships with others. Think of a worrisome circumstance between you and a spouse, close friend, or relative. It could be related to a parent who is too much involved in trying to guide your life, or to a spouse with whom you disagree concerning the best way to discipline the children.

Often these are ongoing stressful situations that you have been thinking about for a long time. Mentally recreate them and, once again, record your thoughts into the tape recorder. Complete the following sentences to help you find "thinking material" for this exercise:

- My husband (boyfriend) makes me furious when he . . .

- My boss is always . . .

- My best friend is a real treasure except when she . . .

- The biggest problem I have with my child (children) is . . .

- My husband's (boyfriend's) biggest fault is that he . . .

- People make me furious when they . . .

- My life would be a lot easier if only . . .

- I just wish my parent(s) would understand that I . . .

These three situations—uncontrolled eating, career stress, and interpersonal stress—will provide the thinking material necessary for you to learn and apply flexibility thinking. You then will be able to monitor and *change* your thoughts as stressful situations occur on a day-to-day basis.

Now that you have recorded your thinking patterns, you have completed Day 1 of the Cognitive Change Module. We told you it was going to be easy!

Chapter 10

THE COGNITIVE
CHANGE MODULE:
DAY 2

*Correcting the Three
Crucial Thinking Mistakes*

*T*he next step toward flexibility thinking involves transcribing your tape-recorded thoughts to your notebook. This written version of your thoughts will serve as your worksheet as you complete the procedures on Day 2. Create a format like the sample below, writing your thoughts on the left side of the page. For now, simply label the right-hand column "Flexibility Thoughts" and leave it blank. You will be writing your thinking corrections in this column.

COGNITIVE CHANGE WORKSHEET

Negative Thoughts   *Flexibility Thoughts*

As you examine your thoughts, you will be looking for the Three Crucial Thinking Mistakes described below. Once you eradicate these particular thinking errors, you will have taken a giant step toward vanquishing the SWEET Syndrome.

As you read about the Three Crucial Thinking Mistakes, look over your worksheet to see if you have made any of these thinking errors. If you recognize one, cross it out, and write a more appropriate thought in the column labeled "Flexibility Thoughts." You will find suggestions on how to formulate more flexible thoughts in the descriptions that follow.

Thinking Mistake #1: "I will achieve happiness and acceptance by being meticulous, precise, and orderly in all aspects of my life."

Perfectionistic all-or-nothing thinking in relation to your appearance, career, eating habits, and relationships with other people is a major underlying cause of the SWEET Syndrome. These extremes of thinking lead to the extremes of behavior and emotion that you experience. You either are eating "perfectly" or you are "bingeing." You are either on top of the world emotionally or you are frustrated and discouraged.

An underlying assumption that most perfectionistic thinkers make is that the only way to be acceptable to themselves and to others is to be perfect. They push themselves to be flawless in appearance, character, and accomplishment. Whenever a job is well done, they examine ways that it could have been done better or faster.

Of course, since we are all human and subject to mistakes, we are all, by definition, less than perfect. Perfection is an impossibility. You may understand this intellectually, but your thoughts and emotions have yet to be convinced. They continue to operate under the misconception that you will achieve happiness and acceptance by being meticulous, precise, and orderly in all aspects of your life.

At the root of this false assumption is all-or-nothing thinking. Especially when under stress, you may perceive people, circumstances, and even yourself as being right or wrong, fair or unfair, successful or unsuccessful, or good or bad. All-or-nothing thinking *narrows your options* in life.

Let's suppose that you are dieting in an attempt to lose a few pounds. One evening after a particularly stressful day, you blow the diet completely. As you examine your thoughts you hear, "I was being so good on my diet. Why did I have to go off it just when I was making progress?"

These thoughts represent not one but two examples of all-or-nothing thinking. First, you are saying that you are "good" when you are dieting and following the rules and that you are "bad" when you are not following your dietary regimen. You may often use the adjectives "good" and "bad" to describe yourself when you are being precise and organized and when you are not. Second, you are telling yourself that there are only two extremes as far as dieting is concerned, namely, being "on" a diet or being "off" a diet. Since there are only two extremes, with no middle ground, even one small slip-up is as bad as an all-out binge.

When all-or-nothing thinking pervades your life, the result is a bit like finding yourself on an emotional roller coaster. You may feel on top of the world one minute and be completely down in the dumps the next. Since eating habits are so responsive to stress levels, it's reasonable to expect that they will parallel this volatile pattern.

Look again at the thoughts you have written down, paying particular attention to any thought that *fails to consider the middle ground*.

Such statements would include:

"I'm totally inadequate. I wish I were able to handle stress as well as others."

"Everything is going wrong this morning. I can tell it's going to be *one of those days.*"

"Well, there I go. I'm off my exercise program again."

"This report is not up to my usual standards. I might as well not even submit it."

These thoughts assume that people either are adequate or inadequate, days either are good or bad, and exercise is an all-or-nothing proposition.

By now it should be fairly clear which of your entries illustrate Thinking Mistake #1—perfectionistic thinking. Your next task is to write a more flexible version of the same idea in the "Flexibility Thoughts" column directly across the page.

As you consider what to write, remember that there are no rigid categories in the world. Imagine every element of your life plotted on a continuum. See the gray areas, not just the black and white. This may be a little difficult at first, because you may not be accustomed to operating this way. What you are really doing is questioning some very basic assumptions you have been using for much of your life in order to make sense out of the world.

As an example, let's reformulate the four perfectionistic thoughts listed above:

"There's no such thing as being *totally* adequate or inadequate. Besides, I can handle stress as well as most people. In fact, as I think about it, I'm able to handle stress *better* than most."

"A lot of things have gone wrong this morning. I'm not going to let myself think that this will be a 'bad' day because of it. There is no such thing as a 'good' day or 'bad' day. Each day has a little of both and I must remind myself of that."

"Just because I missed one day of exercise doesn't mean that I am 'off' my exercise program. It just means that I'm not perfect, that I'm human. It is normal and natural to be less than perfect, and I won't allow myself to use this as an excuse for feeling guilty or for not exercising."

"Even though this report could be better, it is still a very good one. I was a bit rushed with it because of my work load. I'm just being too hard on myself. I never think anything I do is good enough. I'm not going to allow my inflexible thinking to get in the way of this opportunity. Besides, this report is probably better than most of the others that will be submitted. What am I so worried about?"

Rewriting your thoughts is really quite easy once you get the hang of it.

Thinking Mistake #2: "I must be on guard and ready to react strongly to all problems in my life."

It is certainly an asset to be prepared for life's problems as they arise. However, you can also be *too* prepared by being overly sensitive to even small stresses and strains from day to day. Many busy women exhibit this trait because they live and work in a fast-paced, emotionally charged environment.

Psychologists sometimes use the phrase *to catastrophize* to describe this tendency to overreact mentally to problems. That doesn't mean that you throw an emotional fit each time a problem arises. Far from it. Outwardly you may be completely calm. What we are concerned about is *mental* catastrophizing, and how it contributes to your stress level. In your thoughts, you may be turning a minor problem into a major one or a moderate problem into a catastrophe. The inner tension this causes can actually sap your energy for solving the problem.

When you react in this manner, you are allowing emotions to rule rather than intellect. This may cause you to make errors of judgment, which will produce even more stress. It can become a vicious cycle.

Of course, it is not appropriate to be passive when a situation calls for action or assertiveness. But our concern is that you might *expend so much mental energy worrying about small problems that you do not have enough reserves* to handle the really important stresses.

Here are some examples of catastrophizing:

"This is horrible. This is a disaster. What am I going to do?"

"This has ruined everything. I'm at the end of my rope."

"This is the worst thing that's ever happened to me."

Look over your own thoughts to see if you make these thinking mistakes. Write a flexible thought emphasizing concern and a need for vigilance, *but not overreaction*. The thinking mistakes above could be rewritten as follows:

"This is a difficult situation. I'm not sure yet what to do. I'm not going to allow my mind to overreact to this. I *will* find a way to cope with it."

"This is a temporary setback. Everything isn't ruined. I'm a bit unsettled but I'm not beaten. I'm smart enough to come up with a solution."

"Now, wait a minute! This situation is bad but it certainly is *not* the worst thing that has ever happened or that could happen to me. I have to examine this problem rationally. If there is no solution, I'll just have to learn to live with it."

In your daily life, thinking mistakes may occur so quickly and spontaneously that you barely notice them at first. Consider the case of Nancy, a 33-year-old divorced mother of two toddlers. Her thinking mistakes were making her life more stressful than it already was. After a particularly chaotic morning when her baby-sitter arrived an hour behind schedule, causing Nancy to be late for an important meeting, she experienced an acute anxiety attack. In a flash of insight, she caught herself in the midst of Thinking Mistake #2. As she paid attention to her thoughts about the morning's events, she realized that it was her *thoughts*, not events, that were causing her anxiety attack. This is what was going through her mind:

"Oh no! Today is a complete disaster. I have no control of my life. I'll never get that promotion."

With a little practice you, too, will be able to catch your thinking errors as they occur, and overcome a major contributor to the Smart Woman's Excessive Eating Trap.

Thinking Mistake #3: "To be a worthy person, I must please others through my achievements, intellect, and personal appearance."

This thinking mistake puts much of your control over life in the hands of other people. If you are a person who values your independence (and don't we all?), *this thinking mistake will put you in conflict with yourself and others time and time again.*

The conflict arises out of the idea that external factors govern your self-worth. By "external" we mean that your self-concept is determined not by your own evaluation of yourself, but by how others perceive you or value your achievements. For example, Marsha, a copywriter, might think the following about her boss:

"She didn't seem too enthused about my presentation to the sales group. She probably didn't like it. Maybe I'm in the wrong profession."

Not only is Marsha allowing someone else's opinion to dominate her evaluation of herself, but she is also using it to jump to a conclusion that may be false. Perhaps Marsha's boss simply was distracted. Perhaps she was impressed by Marsha's performance but had other things on her mind.

Based on her assumptions, Marsha might go home from work feeling frustrated and depressed and primed for an out-of-control eating episode.

While other people's opinions of you should be taken into consideration in evaluating your self-worth, they should not constitute the *only* criterion by which these evaluations are made. A healthy self-image is derived from a mixture of your own and others' evaluations. You may be giving too much credence to what others think (or what you *believe* they think) and not balancing this with your own judgments.

This thinking mistake may be a long-standing presence in your life. It creates constant pressure for you to look and act perfectly in order to feel good about yourself. Since neither perfection nor 100 percent approval by everyone is possible, this thinking mistake can turn life into an emotional roller coaster ride in which you are happy and full of self-confidence one day and miserable and full of self-doubt the next.

It's important to develop an *internal frame of reference* so that your happiness and self-esteem are based on stable, unchanging beliefs that are impervious to day-to-day events or comments by others.

Amanda is the 28-year-old manager of a popular restaurant in New York City. She is a successful, self-assured woman who earns more than $50,000 a year in salary and bonuses and who has had several lucrative job offers from larger restaurants. However, until recently, despite her very apparent success, her thinking mistakes were causing depression, frustration, and uncontrolled eating episodes. Amanda needed continual external proof of her success in order to feel happy, as well as recognition from others that she was a worthwhile person. During periods when such external feedback was not forthcoming, she experienced a significant drop in confidence. While she kept working and producing in spite of this unhappiness, these emotional lows resulted in outbreaks of out-of-control eating.

A prime example of Thinking Mistake #3 occurred when Amanda and her boyfriend, Fred, ended their relationship after dating for over a year. Fred was an attorney who worked hard every day, but who wanted his home life to be spontaneous and free from routine. Amanda, on the other hand, was a highly organized person. While Fred worked diligently, he always left enough time for social and recreational pursuits. Amanda rarely gave herself any free time. Her career as well as her daily five-mile jogs in the park were extremely important to her.

While their differences at first were a novelty and actually helped to bring them together, they eventually caused much distress, especially to Fred. He complained that he rarely saw Amanda, that she was working too hard. He also claimed that she was selfish in their relationship, always putting her needs before his. Actually, Fred was a very self-centered individual who made a habit of getting his own way by intimidating others. He resented that Amanda did not bow to his wishes.

The breakup of their relationship shocked Amanda deeply. She became depressed, stopped exercising altogether, and her out-of-control eating episodes increased in frequency. When Amanda examined her thinking patterns, this is what she wrote on her Cognitive Change Worksheet:

> "There I go again. I've failed at another relationship. There must be something wrong with me. This just goes to prove that I'm a failure with men. Maybe I *am* selfish. I've never really thought of myself as self-centered, but maybe I am. My life is a wreck. What's the use of exercising and eating right? I can't succeed in my relationships, and I can't succeed in controlling my eating. I have no control over anything in my life."

Once she wrote down her inflexible thinking, Amanda was able to see where she was going wrong. Her logic was, "I failed; therefore, I am a failure" and, "Someone thinks I am selfish; therefore, maybe I am." She was allowing external factors to determine her worth as a person. She was also falling into the trap of all-or-nothing thinking by assuming that if she failed in one relationship, she was a failure in all relationships.

If a child misbehaves and throws a toy car at a playmate, responsible parents are careful to convey to the child that it is her action, not herself as a person, that is unacceptable. It's as if the parent were saying, "While *you* will always be acceptable and loved, some of *your behavior* may not be." This is an important distinction for adults to make in the way they think about themselves.

Amanda was able to write a new set of thoughts based on Flexibility Thinking:

"Basically, I am a successful, loving, honest, and intelligent person. Nothing that anyone does or says can change that fact.

"I may fail at times, but that does not make *me* a failure. I may act in ways some people may consider selfish or uncaring at times, but that does not change the fact that, deep down, I am a caring, loving person. Besides, there are a great many people who value me and my friendship. I have had at least one fulfilling, long-term relationship with a man in the past, and I can do it again."

Use Day 2 to look over your own thoughts for examples of Thinking Mistakes #1, 2, and 3. Reformulate each of them so that you begin to base your self-worth not on achievements or on what others think, but on internal qualities that will always be part of you, no matter what happens.

Chapter

11

THE COGNITIVE CHANGE MODULE: DAYS 3 AND 4

Programming Flexibility Thinking into Your Mind

*N*ow you are ready to program these flexibility thoughts into your mind, a task that comprises Days 3 and 4 of the Hilton Head Program.

First, make certain that you have written a new mental script on your Cognitive Change Worksheet for each of the three situations you analyzed on Day 1. Remember, these included:

1. An out-of-control eating episode

2. A career problem

3. A stressful encounter with a friend, colleague, or relative

Now record each of your new thinking monologues into your tape recorder. Make sure you use words that you are accustomed to using. Flexibility thoughts must sound normal and natural.

The secret to programming your mind with new material is *repetition,* and plenty of it. Listen to this tape recording *three times a day for the next two days.* It is best to listen to the tape by yourself in a quiet moment free from distractions.

It is very important to accept these new thoughts as they are, without changing them. *Do not question flexibility thoughts as you listen to them.* While these new thoughts may seem strange to you at first, if you question them, your mind will not accept them. Hint: Memorize the thoughts and repeat them aloud as if you were practicing a speech. This technique will depersonalize the information and you'll be programming in new thoughts before you know it. It is best to space your listening sessions throughout the day so that you are listening to the tape once in the morning, once in the afternoon, and again in the evening. After you have listened, spend a few quiet minutes going over the thoughts once again in your mind.

Really ponder these new thoughts. Try to recall the *exact words* used on the tape. The case of Justine will illustrate how this is accomplished. Justine is a 27-year-old freelance writer with a master's degree in English literature. Her ambition is to write quality fiction. She is single and lives alone in her small Brooklyn apartment, earning a modest living by writing health and fitness articles for various magazines. She dates occasionally but, being a bit reserved, spends much of her time writing, reading, and working out at a local health club.

Justine's primary thinking mistakes revolved around frustration and depression over periodic, uncontrolled chocolate-eating episodes and all-or-nothing thoughts about her writing career. When confronted with rejection letters from publishers, for example, she would fear that her writing career was over, blame herself for being without talent, and judge herself to be inferior to other writers.

Justine rewrote her negative thought patterns and listened to her flexibility thinking tapes. As she listened, she concentrated intently on what was being said. For example, one flexible thought about a recent rejection of her novel by a prominent publishing firm was:

> "Okay, so I received another rejection letter. I'm not going to take it personally. This has nothing to do with my talent as a writer. Some of the current best-selling authors were rejected many times in the past. Besides, *I* know I'm a good writer whether or not I ever get my book published."

As Justine listened to these words she maintained a positive, upbeat mood. She reinforced these new thoughts by making statements like, "That's right! I am a talented writer!" as she listened. It is important that you become *emotionally involved* in this manner as you listen to your tapes. Cheer yourself on!

When you have completed the 12-day program, you can reinforce the Cognitive Change Module by rewriting negative thoughts associated with other situations in your life. Select problems (even minor ones) that occur in your everyday life, especially those related to eating, marriage, relationships with others, family, and career. Justine extended her newly learned flexibility thinking to such problems as periodic creative blocks with her writing, her reluctance to visit her invalid mother, and her tendency to overdo (to the point of injury) her aerobic exercise routines during times of stress.

To create flexibility thinking about other issues in your life, go through the same steps described previously:

- Tape-record your thoughts about each situation.

- Write these thoughts in the left-hand column of your Cognitive Change Worksheet.

- Identify which of the Three Crucial Thinking Mistakes are causing you to be dominated by your thoughts.

- Write new scripts emphasizing Flexibility Thinking in the right-hand column of your Cognitive Change Worksheet.

- Record your Flexibility Thoughts for each situation into your tape recorder.

- *Actively* listen to the tape, three times a day, for two days.

In time, you will find that flexibility thoughts spontaneously come to your mind as new problems arise. When you engage in negative thinking, your mind will automatically question it and try to reject it.

You may need to do extra work on thoughts associated directly with out-of-control eating episodes. Take careful note of thoughts that occur just prior to, during, and immediately after overeating. Be forewarned that you may not feel like doing this at the time. Your mind may try to fight you, resisting interference with the habitual course of the eating episode.

Crucial Fact #23
The times when you *least* want to examine your thoughts are the times when you *most* need to do so.

If you can catch your thoughts *at the moment* that they occur, and conquer them right then and there, you will have won a major battle: You will have overcome your old way of thinking during one of your most vulnerable times. Changing thoughts as they occur will become easier as you become more and more sensitive to the Three Crucial Thinking Mistakes and can "back off" from your own negative thoughts. Developing flexibility thinking is like developing any other ability: The more you practice, the more proficient you become. The power lies within you. We are merely giving you the tools with which to tap it.

Congratulations! After the first four days of the Hilton Head Program you have completed the Cognitive Change Module. You are already one-third of the way to a new level of effectiveness in your life.

Chapter

12

THE CRAVING CONTROL
LADDER MODULE

Ascending the Craving
Control Ladder

*N*ow that you have begun to overcome the thinking styles at the root of the SWEET Syndrome, you are ready to apply specific craving control techniques that will change your body's *physical* responses to food, enhance your ability to resist temptation, and restore your control over eating.

In Chapter 6 we revealed how negative eating habits develop and the effect that these have on mind and body. In particular, you learned how the body can be conditioned to respond to certain foods and triggering events that cause hunger. Now it's time to change those responses and build your willpower.

Mastering the New Willpower

These techniques are simple skills that will be effective if they are practiced systematically. You will reap their benefits very quickly, but it is important to persevere in order to see lasting results. You would not expect to be able to learn to drive after just one lesson, so why expect to eliminate temptation after one or two craving control sessions? Don't let perfectionistic thinking sabotage your attempts to learn these very simple skills!

Crucial Fact #24
The more energy you put into practicing these techniques, the more you will get out of them.

How Long Does It Take to Change a Habit?

Our clients ask us this question because they sometimes find it difficult to believe that eating habits that may have lasted decades can be changed in a few sessions. The fact is that long-lasting habits, particularly eating habits, often can be changed fairly quickly *precisely because they have become so automatic and unchallenged.* You will develop confidence and optimism in a surprisingly short time. The most frequently noted effect of beginning these exercises is a return of confidence and a feeling that your eating patterns can be controlled. Do not forget that one of the main consequences of this technique is the regaining of both control and confidence.

We also find that the power of this program rests in the fact that, by using it, you learn *how to do the right things rather than how to avoid doing the wrong things.* You are learning a positive way to handle temptation rather than simply trying to avoid it at all costs. Avoidance strategies are not viable long-term techniques because you cannot avoid temptation indefinitely—you need to be able to control it.

Crucial Fact #25
People learn more by trial and *success* than they do by trial and error.

What Is a "Craving?"

A "craving" represents a feeling of being *compelled* to eat certain foods. For most people this feeling of compulsion is stronger in certain situations and for certain foods. It is particularly strong when they most want to resist these temptations.

Craving has very little to do with hunger. Although hunger often will exacerbate a craving situation, most craving episodes occur in response to stress.

Crucial Fact #26
Craving occurs during negative emotional states—when you are angry, tense, upset, bored, depressed.

Most people crave carbohydrates, sweets, or foods with a distinctive taste, either spicy or salty. Ironically, these are also the foods that present the most problems from a weight-control point of view. Very few of our clients have ever expressed a craving for lettuce. Even if they did, it might not present a serious dietary problem for them. Perhaps the only way that lettuce could hurt you would be if a ton of it fell on top of you!

> **Crucial Fact #27**
> **Forbidden fruits are tempting simply because they are forbidden!**

Why do we crave high-calorie carbohydrates and sweets in times of stress? First, these foods represent tasty rewards. They give us a quick boost of satisfaction—just the sort of thing we need when we are suffering from the three H's: hungry, harassed, and hounded! Secondly, stress situations cause us to use up adrenaline. Some researchers believe that carbohydrates are needed to help replenish our supply of this important hormone. Whatever the cause of cravings, it's necessary to gain control of them in order to minimize the physical and emotional discomfort that come with continually giving in to temptation.

The Craving Control Ladder

The Craving Control Ladder is designed to help you confront *increasingly difficult craving situations in a systematic manner.* Each time you confront these situations and resist eating, you are deconditioning those physiological responses which have had such a powerful influence over your behavior.

The Craving Control Ladder is composed of several rungs. Each successive rung represents a set of tasks of increasing difficulty. We call them the Levels of Mastery. In addition, the ladder is divided into three different zones, which represent different types of assignments. These assignments also vary in degree of difficulty.

At the bottom of the ladder are the easier class of assignments. These are the Visualization Exercises described in Chapter 13. They are the easiest to do because they do not involve direct exposure to food. Once you have mastered the visualization exercises, you progress to what we call "Close Encounters," described in Chapter 14. These are situations in which you will come into direct contact with your favorite foods. At the top of the ladder are the Tasting Exercises outlined in Chapter 15. These involve actually tasting small amounts of your favorite foods.

In the next three chapters we will outline the procedures for each of the three zones of the Craving Control Ladder. The craving control exercises are designed to:

- Decondition your physical responses

- Improve your ability to resist temptation

- Restore confidence and control

Strategies for Learning by Trial and Success

As you ascend the Craving Control Ladder, you will find that your physical and mental responses toward food are changing. As this happens, keep in mind the following points:

1. The program of exercises is *individualized*. Although the principles of the program are general, the specific exercises will be unique to you, shaped by the situations which trigger the SWEET Syndrome and by the foods that you crave. Although many people crave similar foods and share certain stress experiences, no two people are exactly alike, and many quite different in their tastes and behaviors. If ice cream is not a "danger food" for you, there is little point spending time practicing your ability to resist it. In the examples that follow we will refer to foods that are commonly craved, but these are only examples. You will be shown how to adapt the procedures to the foods that give *you* the most trouble.

2. The exercises are *self-paced*. On the 12-day program, we guide you up the ladder very quickly so you can get a feel for the total program. Once you have gone through the 12-day course, however, it is crucial to return to the rung of the ladder on which you feel most comfortable. Then, work your way up the Craving Control Ladder at a controlled pace. The most important aspect of the program is that you choose exercises which challenge you and *push you to the*

limit but not past it. Only you can be the judge of this. On some days you will have more confidence than on others. This is to be expected. Just remember the basic principle of tackling only those situations which you feel you can conquer. You do not want to make the tasks too easy, because this would not present you with enough challenge. Neither do you want to make the assignments so difficult that you cannot achieve them. Remember, you will learn more by trial and *success* than by trial and error. In Chapter 19 you will find guidance on what to do if you run into difficulties with the Craving Control assignments.

3. *Give yourself credit* for successfully completing an assignment. Sometimes our clients dismiss their achievements and minimize their progress. One reason is that progress is often so swift and dramatic that people cannot believe that it's actually happening! Shirley, a boutique owner, had a terrific penchant for doughnuts. She made two trips to the doughnut shop daily—once in the morning en route to work and again at lunchtime, eating as many as six per day. After working her way up the Craving Control Ladder, one of Shirley's assignments was to sit for ten minutes in her favorite doughnut shop, ordering only a cup of coffee. Having done this successfully, however, Shirley began to minimize her success. She adopted a thinking style in which she said, "If I can do it, it couldn't have been difficult to begin with. Therefore, I have not really achieved anything." Yet only two days earlier, Shirley had told us that successfully completing this task would be a great achievement! So here is a tip for defeating self-defeating thinking:

Before you do each task, rate on a scale of 1 to 10 how much of an achievement you will consider it to be if you successfully complete the task. Then you will be less inclined to minimize your progress and more likely give yourself the credit you deserve. *The better you feel about your performance, the better your performance will be.*

In the next chapter you'll find the visualization exercises that comprise the first rung on the ladder. Good luck!

Chapter 13

THE CRAVING CONTROL LADDER MODULE: DAYS 5 AND 6

Visualizations

The first step on the Craving Control Ladder enables you to visualize yourself successfully resisting temptation in a variety of situations.

How Visualization Helps You Resist Food Temptation

Research has shown that seeing yourself perform an action in your mind's eye increases the likelihood that you will perform that action in a real-life situation. It would appear that mental practice is almost as good as the real-life event. Research also suggests that mental practice can even produce changes in your nervous system. This implies that learning is taking place even though this rehearsal is mental rather than physical.

Imagining success is important because it fosters a "can-do" attitude. After all, *if you can't imagine yourself doing something, the chances are high that you will not do it in reality*. Therefore, it's vital that you think positively about your ability to exercise your New Willpower. Visualization exercises will help you accomplish this, and will set the stage for long-term success, as research in this area shows.

Visualization exercises also help you to gauge what your emotional responses are likely to be in the actual situation. You will be able to anticipate how you are going to feel as you resist your favorite foods. Many of our clients learn through visualization that initially they feel angry or frustrated when they resist foods they really want. Being able to anticipate their emotional response allows them to plan special tactics to handle this when they confront the actual situation and put their New Willpower into practice. They may plan to exercise, telephone a friend, listen to music, or do some other activity that is incompatible with the feeling of frustration immediately after their planned confrontation with food.

The best aspect of these visualization exercises is that they *maximize your ability to resist while minimizing the temptation*. However, do not be deceived into thinking that you will not be tempted! A good visualization exercise *should* engender thoughts and feelings that are very similar, if not identical, to those that you experience in the real-life situation.

Visualization is a mental activity that everyone can do. It's simply a guided form of daydreaming. Even those few people who initially have difficulty imagining specific scenes improve with a little practice.

The Visualization Script

When you are doing these visualization exercises, follow these important guidelines:

- Find some space away from distraction and interruption.

- Make yourself as comfortable as possible. Loosen any tight clothing; take off your shoes.

- Make the room as dark as possible and close your eyes.

Think of a favorite "danger" food that might be available in your own kitchen. You are going to use that food in this example. Having chosen that food, read through the following scene. Concentrate on it carefully, because once you have read it you are going to visualize it. Remember that this is a generic scene designed to have general appeal. Do not worry if the scene described is not personally meaningful. You will have the opportunity to devise your own scenes to visualize a little later. For now, concentrate on this scene:

You arrive home after a hectic day. It's eight o'clock and you have already had something to eat for your evening meal. You are alone and have nothing scheduled for the rest of the evening. You are feeling at a loose end and are a little bored. Before long, your thoughts focus on that favorite food that you know is in your kitchen. Concentrate on that feeling. Despite your attempts to forget about the food, you feel compelled to have some, and you find yourself in your kitchen. Visualize your kitchen in detail. You are starting to feel hungry. Imagine how that feels. See yourself going over to where the food is kept. Imagine getting the food out and carrying it to the table. Visualize the food as you unwrap it. You can almost taste it. Concentrate on that feeling of really wanting this food. *You do not eat it, however*. Instead, imagine yourself taking the food to the sink or trash and throwing it away. Concentrate on how you feel after you have done this.

Spend several minutes visualizing this scene as vividly as possible. It is particularly important to focus on your feelings of craving. How do you feel physically? What thoughts enter your mind? Such cravings will be generated just by doing these exercises. Concentrate on the food, too. See it. Smell it. Notice its texture. You will probably find yourself salivating or tensing up as your body produces its conditioned hunger responses. Take special note of how you feel as you dispose of the food.

Once you have visualized this scene, use your notebook to make the following assessments:

- *Ease of resisting*. Rate how easy it was for you to throw the food away using a scale from 1 to 10, in which 1 represents very easy and 10 very difficult.

148

- *Tension level.* Rate how anxious you felt, using the same ten-point scale.

- Write down any observations you have about your *feelings or thoughts.* For example, are you feeling angry, resentful, or pleased? Note those thoughts. Perhaps you are saying to yourself, "Next time I may not be able to do it," or, "I think I really could do that in the actual situation."

Use the rating scales whenever you do any craving control assignment, including all visualization exercises that follow.

Creating Your Own Powerful Images

Now it's time for you to create personally meaningful scenes to work on. Devise *at least three* typical scenes which represent difficult craving situations for you. These scenes should involve both the *situations* and the *foods* that give you the most trouble. Here are some examples that might help:

The Restaurant   You are at a business lunch with one of your clients. Visualize the client and the restaurant clearly. You have controlled your eating very well during the main part of the lunch, but now the waitress asks if you would like some dessert and shows you a tray of delicious pastries and pies. Your favorite dessert is on it. It's there right in front of you. Your client is urging you to have some, but part of you really wants to resist it. Concentrate on your client's pressure. Imagine what your client is telling you. Imagine feeling under pressure, not wanting to eat it, but not wanting to say no to the urgings of your client. Now see that dessert. Focus on the parts that you really like and how it would feel if you ate it. Then hear yourself declining the offer and deciding against dessert by saying no. Imagine yourself refusing the offer politely but confidently.

The Argument   You arrive home after a busy day. The moment you walk in the door the telephone rings. It's a member of your family (or a friend) whom you sometimes find difficult to deal with. Before long there is a disagreement and you are arguing. You feel yourself getting very agitated. The conversation is terminated unsatisfactorily and you are left feeling angry and frustrated. You find yourself automatically heading for your favorite food. Concentrate on that feeling! See that food! Imagine holding the food and feeling *compelled* to eat it. Then visualize putting (or throwing) the food away. Imagine successfully resisting the temptation.

Shopping   You are out shopping in your favorite store. It is hot and very crowded and you have been shopping for a couple of hours. You are feeling very tired. Suddenly you happen to find yourself passing your favorite ice-cream parlor. You go inside. You can see your favorite ice cream right there in front of you. Imagine that ice cream. Concentrate on your feeling of tiredness and on the temptation.

Then see yourself successfully resisting and buying only a diet soda.

If you are still struggling to create meaningful scenes, just remember actual "craving" situations or incidents that have happened in the past and adapt them to the visualization routine.

Ascending the Five Levels of Mastery

Now that you have constructed your scenes, you're ready to practice them systematically. Remember that your aim is to start off easy and increase the level of mastery as you accomplish the easier steps. Here are some ways of making the visualization exercises easy to begin with:

- Practice the assignments when you are very relaxed. Two good times might be before going to bed, or when soaking in a hot tub.

- Practice the assignments when you are not hungry.

- Practice the assignments in a place that is far removed from the temptation. If you are practicing at home, it is a good idea not to have your favorite foods on hand.

These conditions represent the first of five Levels of Mastery. As you practice these visualizations, you will find that you feel more and more comfortable imagining them. You also will find it easier to envision yourself resisting temptation, as your rating scales will show. We recommend that you spend two days working on these five mastery levels and getting acquainted with the techniques before moving on to the next chapter. Subsequently you may need to return to the visualization exercises to achieve complete mastery. In fact, you will probably feel most comfortable practicing these visualizations periodically to keep affirming your mastery over tempting foods.

To make the exercises more challenging, simply change some of the circumstances under which you practice these visualizations. The circumstances that represent increasing levels of challenge are:

Level 1:   Practice visualizations when relaxed, not hungry, and your tempting food is not easily available.

Level 2:   Practice visualizations when tempting food is readily available.

Level 3:   Practice visualizations when you are hungry.

Level 4:   Practice visualizations when you are not relaxed.

Level 5:   Practice visualizations when you are hungry, stressed, and the tempting food is available.

Be sure to change *only one* of these parameters at a time. Talk yourself out of a perfectionistic push to test yourself in a difficult situation before you are ready. Don't be in a rush!

Practice Recap.   In this chapter you have:

- Learned how to prepare for visualization techniques

- Learned how to monitor and rate your performance

- Devised at least three "craving" scenes that are relevant to you

- Learned how to ascend the five Levels of Mastery

Now, spend the remainder of Days 5 and 6 practicing your visualizations. Move as far up the Craving Control Ladder as feels comfortable. Don't worry if you have not achieved complete mastery by the end of Day 6. The purpose of these two days of practice is to acquaint you with the techniques rather than push you. You can return to them later. Even if you have not completed all five levels, you can still proceed to Close Encounters, Days 7 and 8, in the next chapter.

Chapter 14

THE CRAVING CONTROL LADDER MODULE: DAYS 7 AND 8

Close Encounters

We call the exercises in this chapter Close Encounters because, using them, you will systematically come into direct contact with your danger situations and your favorite foods *without eating them*.

If possible, try to avoid your "craving" situations except when doing these conditioning module assignments. Of course, this is not always feasible. If you are unavoidably confronted with these situations before you are ready, simply approach each one as a challenge and do your best. Remember, each time you successfully confront a difficult "craving" situation, your confidence will increase.

How to Confront Your Favorite Foods and Win

You are going to be working on the "craving" situations that are most challenging for you, in increasingly difficult increments. Along the way you will be rating your performance so you can assess progress.

First, write in your notebook at least three difficult "craving" situations. These may be similar to, or even identical to, the ones you used for your visualizations. It is not important whether or not they are different. The main point is that they are situations that present you with difficulty and trigger responses which you wish to change.

To help you devise your confrontation strategy, bear in mind that each "craving" situation is made up of a few key parts. Analyze the following characteristics of your three "craving" situations and write your assessments in your notebook:

- *The food itself.* As we discussed earlier, it is only certain foods, or categories of food, that are involved in your cravings. You know which of these are your "danger" foods. Write down which foods you crave and their characteristics.

- *Places.* The SWEET Syndrome often occurs only in certain places. The kitchen may seem the obvious environment, but this is by no means always the case. Joan, a Boston attorney, was a fairly typical example of a late-night eater who would retire to her bedroom at the end of a long day with a book and her favorite cookies. Others overeat only when watching television or while reading in their favorite armchair. Most out-of-control eating occurs in very private places. Judy, a Midwest executive, would buy her favorite foods and then drive to the outskirts of town, where she could sit in the privacy of her car in a secluded spot and eat without fear of being seen. Many eating episodes occur in cars. Of course, eating food in the places in which they are bought, such as ice-cream parlors, delis, and patisseries, is widespread. Write down where your overeating episodes occur.

- *Time.* Many out-of-control eating episodes occur at specific times. The most frequent times are in the late afternoon, in the middle of the evening, and the last thing before bedtime. Be aware of your "danger" times, and write them in your notebook.

- *Mood.* As we have noted, negative mood states are most frequently associated with out-of-control eating. Write down which moods make you particularly susceptible to overeating.

Varying each of these components will affect the difficulty of your assignment. Your favorite doughnuts might be easier to resist if they are confronted at a different time or place than that in which they are normally eaten. A word of caution, however: It is important not to underestimate the power of the food itself. You may think that it will be easy to resist your favorite foods when you confront them in situations in which you don't normally eat them, but you may be surprised at how powerful an effect the food alone has.

Take the case of Katherine, an accountant in her forties. We proposed that she sit in the "neutral zone" of our office and come face to face with her favorite candy bar in our presence. She thought this would be easy. It was not her habit to overeat in front of others. She agreed to do the assignment even though she thought that it would not present her with enough challenge.

Katherine was in a good mood when she began the assignment. Within a few minutes, however, she was completely overwhelmed and actually was in tears. The chocolate bar was extremely tempting to her. She felt that it controlled her. She desperately wanted to eat it. Her feeling of helplessness made Katherine tearful and depressed. The exercise showed her that even in situations that were quite removed from her usual eating habits, the food exerted an enormously strong effect by itself. Katherine was able to negotiate the Craving Control Ladder successfully, aided enormously by this experience which helped her to appreciate how much control this particular food had over her.

Crucial Fact #28
You can still experience strong craving
even in situations which seem far removed
from your usual eating scenarios.

Having drawn up your "craving" situations, the next step is to break them down into *degrees of difficulty*. Let's use the nocturnal eating of Joan, mentioned above, as an example.

Joan's out-of-control eating occurred mainly at home, typically in the late evening, on a weeknight, while she was in bed. The cookies were nearly always chocolate-chip. She noted these key elements of her "craving" situation in her notebook. In her Close Encounters assignments, we varied the time and place of her eating as well as the food itself in order to alter the difficulty of the task.

We could have asked Joan not to confront chocolate-chip cookies in her assignments and had her replace them with something less tempting, like raw vegetables or even less-favored cookies. We did not recommend this because Joan felt that anything less than the "real McCoy" would present her with no challenge. Had she not thought this, we would have recommended starting the exercises with a less-favored cookie.

Joan devised an initial close encounter that consisted of the following elements:

- Chocolate-chip cookies

- At home during the day on a weekend

- For five minutes

- When not hungry or stressed

When constructing your exercises, use your notebook to *itemize the elements of the "craving" situation* as shown above. This helps you to identify the aspects of the situation that can be changed to increase the difficulty of the task.

When Joan had mastered this scenario, she progressed to a five-minute exposure to the cookies on a weekday evening—although not late at night and not in her bedroom. When she had mastered this assignment, she progressed to having the cookies in her bedroom, though not at her bedside, when she was reading at night.

Finally, she was able to place the cookies at her bedside while reading and successfully resist them.

Joan asked us whether it was advisable to eat different foods at bedtime to replace the cookies once she felt she had mastered the situation. It can be useful to substitute different foods to vary the difficulty of the assignment while climbing the Craving Control Ladder. The substitution of foods as a long-term coping strategy, however, is not a good idea, no matter how "healthy" the substitute foods are.

Most of our clients tell us that food substitutions are not very successful. Typically, they do not enjoy the food or find it satisfying. For this reason, food substitutions often turn out to be food *additions*. People eat the "healthy" substitution, and—when that does not satisfy them—they eat the favored food as well!

Secondly, remember that the entire point of these exercises is to train your body *not to expect food*. Consequently, any eating in the situation runs counter to the point of this program.

Meet the Challenge, Increase Your Confidence

Now, take each of your "craving" situations and break them down into tasks of increasing difficulty. In doing so, note two other key ways to vary the difficulty of the assignment:

- Increase the *amount of time* you spend confronting the situation. Your assignment could last from a few seconds to a few hours.

- Incorporate the *presence of others*. Because most out-of-control eating occurs when you are alone, the presence of others often makes it easier to resist temptation that might be almost irresistible if you were on your own. Use others as a source of support and a way of making assignments easier. Inform them about the principles of the program and let them help you design your assignments. Use them for support during the assignments. Involve them in the monitoring of your behavior by asking them to help you rate your performance.

You are ready to tackle these assignments, working from the easiest up. Remember to use the rating scales mentioned in the previous chapter:

- Before doing each exercise, rate on a scale of 1 to 10 how much of an achievement it would be to complete the assignment successfully.

- Using the 1 to 10 scale, rate how easy or difficult it is to resist temptation, and rate your level of anxiety. Take these measurements at the beginning and at the end of the assignment.

- Make any other relevant observations about the assignment and your responses.

Troubleshooting Tips

Because you are putting yourself in increasingly high-risk situations, there is always the chance that you will not be able to resist temptation and that you will eat the craved foods. Surprisingly, this does not seem to happen very much on the Hilton Head Program, but it is a possibility. If you do eat the food, here is what to do:

- Realize that you should not be too surprised. After all, you are deliberately creating scenarios that evoke your desire to eat.

- Do not feel guilty or bad about your setback. It probably indicates that in your eagerness to eradicate the SWEET Syndrome, you have set yourself too difficult an assignment. Eagerness is not something to feel guilty about. You are taking steps to tackle the problem and it's important to keep your performance in perspective. Do not fall back into an all-or-nothing, self-punishing thinking style!

- Re-examine the assignment and determine what made it more difficult than you thought it would be. Have you underestimated the power of any of the elements in the situation? You might need to redesign the assignment. It may entail too much of a jump in difficulty from the previous one. Construct a task of intermediate difficulty.

- In any event, return to and repeat the previously

mastered task on your ladder. Once you feel comfortable with that assignment, climb back up the ladder.

Keep practicing these exercises until you feel in control of your danger foods and situations. As you get more confident, you might want to have foods around the house that you previously have avoided buying, as a continuing test of your resolve. Several of our clients have deliberately bought their favorite cookies or chocolates and left them prominently on display so that they could constantly exert their New Willpower, and congratulate themselves for doing so!

When you have mastered the Close Encounters, you are very near the top of the Craving Control Ladder. You have just a few more rungs to climb.

Chapter 15

THE CRAVING CONTROL LADDER MODULE: DAY 9

The Tasting Exercises

*I*f you intend to eat any of those craved foods again, you want to be able to eat them in moderation. The exercises you have completed so far have been designed to show you that you have the ability to *resist* eating these foods. There are two aspects, however, to successfully controlling any addictive or compulsive problem, including out-of-control eating. The first aspect is learning to *resist* the temptation. This you have now learned to do. The second aspect involves dealing successfully with a situation in which you find yourself having *already eaten* a small amount of that "danger" food. Many programs are very good at addressing the avoidance of food, but not so good at providing treatment designed to help once you have already taken that first step of consuming the forbidden item. The Tasting Exercises will help whether you intend to eat your "danger" foods in moderation or even if you intend never to eat them again.

Taking the Conflict Out of Eating

It is important to realize the distinction between eating foods in moderate amounts when you *choose* to do so and bingeing on them infrequently. Any bingeing, no matter how infrequent, could lead to the redevelopment of negative eating habits. Because you do not want to deprive yourself of your favorite foods, it is important to learn to eat them in moderation. Besides, the business of daily life tends to put the foods we crave within easy reach.

Some people do make a serious commitment to avoid completely foods that have given them problems. This is okay as long as it is feasible. However, our experience is that people who make a commitment to avoid *commonly available* foods ultimately have difficulty with these foods again. Moreover, they are often making this commitment from a position of helplessness. In effect they are still saying, "There is nothing I can do to control my reaction to these foods; therefore, I must simply avoid them." This attitude betokens that dangerous all-or-nothing thinking style that can lead to self-punishing bingeing. If you make this commitment you are constantly walking a tightrope, living with the fear that you may topple off at any moment.

If you do decide to avoid certain foods, this program will help you do so from *a position of strength*. If you know you have the ability to exercise control over these foods, they will not appear so appealing and cause you to question your resolve if exposed to them. Moreover, you will be more likely to avoid them effectively if you have mastered your behavior toward them. So whether it is your intention to eat your foods in moderation or to avoid them altogether, the Tasting Exercises are essential to meeting your goals.

The Tasting Exercises: Food Fire Drills

Look upon these exercises as fire drills that will help protect you in times of emergency. If you have practiced limiting your consumption of your favorite foods successfully, these will help you enormously if you should find yourself indulging beyond your intentions. And it is crucial to recognize that it is likely that at some point you will find yourself wanting to overindulge in those favorite foods again. It won't happen very frequently, or to the same extent as before, but you would be less than human if you did not have a minor "slip" from time to time. After all, haven't we established that you—like everyone else—are not perfect? (In a future chapter we will provide information on how to handle slip-ups.)

Day 9 involves doing *three* tasting exercises, which you will practice until you feel you have mastered them completely. Progress at your own pace, taking on tasks that challenge but do not overwhelm you.

Because you actually will be eating a small amount of your favorite food, it is possible that your desire for further eating will be stimulated, or "primed." That is what makes these exercises both more interesting and challenging. To help deal with this possible priming effect, bear in mind the following suggestions:

- Plan something to do *immediately after* these tasting assignments. If you are occupied, it will be easier to set aside any desire to continue eating. Your planned activity should be something you enjoy doing and obviously should not be food-related. Some form of physical activity, like exercise or yard work, or something relaxing, like listening to music, soaking in a hot tub, or phoning a friend, are activities that have been used successfully by our clients.

- At first, practice these Tasting Exercises in the absence of your "craving" foods. If cookies are a "danger" food, don't have any of them easily available (apart from the one you will be using as part of the tasting exercise). As you gain confidence, danger foods should be made available both during and after your food tasting.

- Initially, do these assignments in the presence of another, informed, supportive person. Make sure anyone who helps you with the exercises understands the purpose of the assignments and what you are trying to do.

- Do not undertake these assignments when you are overly stressed or excessively hungry. In fact, we would recommend that you *never* eat your danger foods in the presence of stress or any negative emotion. One reason why these particular foods became so dangerous is that they have been serving as comforters. It is important not to slip back into that habit. If possible, you should not eat *at all* when overstressed. Similarly, do not indulge in your "craving" foods at a time of extreme hunger, when your control naturally will be weaker.

Working Through the Tasting Exercises

First, write down at least three of your favorite foods. Ensure that there are some foods on the list that are not your absolute favorites, but ones in which you do indulge. Rank the foods from most to least preferred (even the least preferred will be one that still tempts you.) You are going to start these Tasting Exercises with the lowest preference on your list. *Do not underestimate the power of this food, even though it is not your absolute favorite.* As you gain confidence with the foods on the bottom of the list, you will progress to the more difficult-to-resist foods. Consider how Carla, a features editor for a national women's magazine, constructed her first tasting exercises for Day 9 of the program. Carla, who is in her early thirties, has struggled with food since she began her job at the magazine three years ago. Her penchant was salty, savory foods. She would overindulge on cheese and crackers and often craved pizza, but her absolute favorites were roasted peanuts. Carla's notebook showed her ranked preferences like this:

1. Roasted peanuts

2. Pepperoni pizza

3. Crackers and cheddar cheese

Having ranked her foods, Carla was ready to start the tasting exercise, using crackers and cheese as the first test.

The Tasting Exercise consists of eating a small amount of the test food. A "small amount" means just that: a small amount. The test food could be one small cookie, half a regular-sized bar of chocolate, a small scoop of ice cream, half a slice of bread with a modest amount of peanut butter, and so on. In Carla's case she took one saltine cracker and put a small square of her favorite cheese on it. We told Carla to keep any "danger" food, except for the portion of test food, well out of the way. Carla opted for buying a small packet of crackers and throwing all but the test cracker away. Similarly, she had bought only a small amount of cheddar cheese, and had given what she did not need for the tasting exercise to a friend. Some foods can be bought in small amounts; others require more planning. Don't make it difficult for yourself by having a quantity of your favorite food available when the tasting exercise may have primed you to eat. If you do have your favorite foods available, keep them out of reach by giving them to someone else, either to stock for you or to eat. Alternatively, you could always throw away any excess test food. More about that later.

Smell the test food. Lick it several times to get the flavor. Observe your reactions to it. Carla became masterful at the tasting exercises. She would hold the cracker and focus on it for about a minute. Having examined it, she would then smell it for about thirty seconds. Immediately after this, she would jot her reactions in her workbook, using the ten-point scale mentioned earlier. A sample record from her workbook looked like this:

Day 9   Tasting Exercise #3   Cracker & Cheese

Smelling cracker

    Desire to eat   7

    Difficulty resisting 5

    Anxiety   3

Thoughts: A little easier. I know I'm going to resist eating this.

Having smelled the cracker and recorded her reactions, Carla would then lick the cracker. She would taste the saltiness of the cracker and the distinct, pungent taste of the cheddar cheese. After she had licked the cracker three times she would record her reactions to doing so:

    Licking cracker

        Desire to eat   8

        Difficulty resisting 5

        Anxiety   3

Thoughts: Not as difficult as I imagined.

Having done this, Carla then ate the cracker *slowly,* focusing on the taste. *Do not eat the test food in one or two quick bites in a matter of seconds!* Eating the food slowly during the tasting exercises and savoring its taste increases your awareness of its strong taste-cues, which is vital in helping you understand what triggers your wish to eat this particular food.

Having eaten the test food, record your observations. Here is Carla's record immediately after having eaten the cracker:

Eaten cracker

Desire to eat	6
Difficulty resisting	3
Anxiety	2

Thoughts: Definitely getting easier. I feel good about being able to have just one cracker and stop.

You can see that Carla's desire to eat diminished after having eaten the cracker. She did not feel tempted to continue eating, and she rated herself as having little difficulty in resisting. Her anxiety had decreased, too. Such record-keeping enabled Carla to quantify her performance and made her progress more tangible.

Once the Tasting Exercise is completed, get involved immediately in another activity. Carla typically went for a walk once she had completed her assignments. Avoid eating *anything* for one hour after the test.

Because these Tasting Exercises might influence your desire to eat for a while after you have finished the assignment, keep a record in your notebook of any notable responses that occur after the exercise. For example, for about an hour after her first two tasting exercises, Carla noted that she felt unusually hungry. This effect faded rapidly after her third tasting exercise. By then she had gained confidence in her ability to master this technique.

On Day 9 of the 12-day program, attempt *three* Tasting Exercises. Do one assignment at a time, allowing at least four hours between each one. Never exceed three Tasting Exercises per day, and always allow at least four hours between each assignment. Until you attain complete mastery of your "craving" foods, they should be eaten only as part of the Tasting Exercises. Do not eat them at any other time during this period.

New Challenges to Try

After completing the initial 12-day program, you can increase the difficulty of the Tasting Exercises in the following ways:

- Choose *more tempting* foods. Carla did not find pizza, second on her list of favorites, particularly difficult to resist. Much to her surprise, she discovered that just three tasting assignments over two days gave her complete confidence to resist pizza. She then moved on to her favorite food: roasted peanuts. It took her six tasting assignments over a period of four days to feel in control of the peanuts.

- Increase the *availability* of the craving foods both during and after testing. In her later tasting exercises, Carla ate half a dozen peanuts and then sat reading for an hour, surrounded by two open cans full of her all-time favorites. When she was able to resist eating in that situation she knew she was ready for . . .

THE ULTIMATE TEST: Take a small amount of your favorite craving food. Cut the food in half. Eat one half and then throw the other half away.

Life at the Top of the Ladder

Now that you have reached the top of the Craving Control Ladder and are exercising good control over your "danger" foods and situations, stay alert to them! Continue to see your encounters with difficult situations as challenges to your self-control that need to be met. Continue to practice the exercises and use the situations that crop up in everyday life as exercises in resistance. Once Carla had reached the top of the Craving Control Ladder and had passed the ultimate test, she approached many of the situations that had previously given her trouble as challenges. She actually looked forward to business lunches as tests of her self-control and confidence. Once you have mastered the Craving Control Ladder, you will not feel apprehensive about high-risk situations, but like Carla, will see them as just another opportunity to exercise and sharpen your skills.

One last thing needs to be said now that you have reached the top of the Craving Control Ladder: Congratulations! You have developed your willpower to the point where it is *you* who controls the food, not the other way around. Well done!

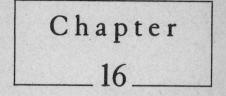

Chapter 16

THE LIFESTYLE BALANCING MODULE: DAY 10

*How to Calculate
Your Happiness Quotient*

Now that you have developed flexibility thinking and have successfully climbed the Craving Control Ladder, only one module of the Hilton Head Program remains. The Lifestyle Balancing Module is designed to provide a symmetry to your life, to eradicate the stresses that can trigger the SWEET Syndrome.

Obligations Versus Pleasures

Psychologists have known for years that the secret to a happy, fulfilling life lies in achieving a balance between your obligations and your pleasures. Let's try a little experiment. Divide a blank page in your notebook into equal halves by drawing a line down the middle. Label the left-hand column with the word *Obligations* and the right-hand column with *Pleasures*.

Under the *Obligations* column, write all of the things you do every day because you feel that you *should* or *need* to do them. These are your duties and responsibilities. For example, you work long hours for income and career satisfaction. Even though you might enjoy many aspects of your work, your career would still be considered an obligation. In other words, you consider it a necessity in your life because it fulfills a physical and/or psychological need. Other obligations might include caring for loved ones, watching your weight, reading career-related material, or attending networking functions.

Now, consider the *Pleasures*. This column should contain all of the things you do each day just for yourself and nobody else. These are the personal pleasures in life. For the most part, these should be activities that bring you an *immediate* sense of enjoyment and satisfaction. They don't have to be healthy or do anyone any good. This list should include activities that are self-centered and even frivolous.

Obviously, some activities during the day may not fit into either category. They may be neutral or may fit into both categories. You may not consider them either obligations or pleasures. If you watch television for an hour in the evening, you might feel that this activity is merely a way to pass the time. Perhaps, only when you are viewing something very special, would you consider it a pleasurable activity.

In your lists of *Obligations* and *Pleasures* include only activities that are part of your current life. For example, do not list pleasurable activities that you want to do or plan to do in the future but are not yet doing. It is important to record your life as it really is, not as you would like it to be.

Michele, a single, 33-year-old advertising executive from Chicago, completed her list as follows:

Obligations	*Pleasures*

Obligations

- Work to expand my career

- Socialize with prospective clients

- Be active in my college alumnae association

- Do volunteer work at center for battered women

- Telephone or visit my mother every week

- Go to my aerobics class three times a week

- Count calories to keep my weight under control

- Read fitness magazines

- Read publications from the advertising industry to keep track of what the competition is doing

Pleasures

- Eat ice cream and cookies late at night

- Go skiing once a year

- Date interesting men (only about once a month because of my busy schedule)

Obligations	*Pleasures*

- Have occasional meals with my associates at the office

- In my spare time, develop new, creative ideas for our accounts

- Travel on business

The trouble with an *Obligations/Pleasures* list like Michele's is that her day-to-day duties far outweigh satisfying diversions. In addition, of the three pleasures listed, the first one, "eating ice cream and cookies late at night," is an activity that, while pleasurable, is unhealthy if it occurs too frequently. In the long run, this is not actually a true pleasure for Michele, because the weight gain causes stress for her.

The other two activities occur so infrequently as to leave Michele practically devoid of any activity that provides real, immediate satisfaction.

The Happiness Formula

In working with clients at the Hilton Head Health Institute, we have found that there is no optimum ratio of obligations to pleasures that results in a balanced life. By "balanced life" we mean one in which you feel relatively satisfied and happy. You feel that life is worth the effort, not just in terms of future rewards, but in the present-day pleasures it offers you. Your pleasures can be counted on and don't depend on the events of your career or the emotional ups and downs of life itself.

We developed the *happiness formula* below to calculate how balanced an individual's life really is:

$$\text{Happiness Quotient} = \frac{\text{Pleasures}}{\text{Obligations}} \times 100$$

To give you an example, let's calculate Michele's happiness quotient from her list above. She had a total of 12 obligations that occurred on a regular basis, at least once a week or more. Only one of her three pleasures would qualify as a regular activity.

In applying this formula, use only *frequently occurring* activities. If Michele gave full credit for an activity that she undertook only rarely, such as "skiing once a year," we would end up with a very distorted picture of her lifestyle.

Here is the sample calculation for Michele:

$$\frac{1}{12} \times 100 = 8.33$$

Michele's happiness quotient is 8.33, a very low score, indicating an unbalanced life consisting of a *great deal of effort and output and very little pleasure and input*. We have found that the optimum happiness quotient for busy women lies between 25 and 40. This range indicates that if your pleasures amount to between 25 percent and 40 percent of your obligations, you probably will feel quite satisfied with your life. It also indicates that your life is in balance, so that stress or crisis in one area will be compensated for by other areas of living.

If your quotient is lower than 25, your life is definitely out of balance. You are fulfilling your self-imposed and other-imposed duties from day to day, but you are not nearly as emotionally fulfilled as you could be.

Crucial Fact #29
The more day-to-day, non-food pleasures
you have, the less important eating
becomes.

It is interesting to note that it is actually possible to develop a happiness quotient that is too high. Too much pleasure without adequate responsibility, hard work, and challenge can be boring and frustrating. You might be able to enjoy this situation for a short time, such as on a vacation, but you would feel unhappy and unfulfilled if it continued for very long.

Hans Selye, one of the major leaders in research on stress management, once observed of stress-prone business executives that if you are a "racehorse" you must run and run and face challenges every day. If, on the other hand, you are a "turtle," you must go at a relaxed, steady pace. If your personality is basically of the "racehorse" variety, trying to turn you into a "turtle" will only frustrate you. You must continue to run, but know when to pace yourself and when to go back to the stable for a rest.

Based on your own list of obligations and pleasures, take a few moments to calculate your happiness quotient. Don't worry if your score is quite low. When clients first come to us, most score between 0 and 15. Our goal is to help you raise your score to the optimum range. This process involves goal-setting and cultivating time-management skills.

Isn't Work Reward Enough?

You may wonder why work itself is not enough to give you pleasure in life. Many women we counsel assert that they really enjoy work, and that most of their pleasure comes from their career. That may be true, but enjoyment of your work is not enough for total happiness and personal adjustment for two reasons.

First, if all of your personal satisfaction is derived from work—only one element in life—the foundation of your happiness is weak. Everything rests on a single linchpin. Because of this lack of diversity, a bad day at work will leave you devastated. You will have nothing else to fall back on. It's a bit like investing all of your money in one stock and watching the stock rise and fall on a daily basis. You are emotionally at the mercy of the element of volatility. You may have everything to gain—but you also have everything to lose.

Since enjoyment from career activities is such a fluctuating commodity, you will be vulnerable to using food for pleasure and stress reduction.

Second, no matter how much satisfaction you derive from work, it doesn't compare to the elemental physical and psychological pleasure derived from more frivolous "play" activities. According to Dr. George Sheehan, physician and sports writer, the ability to enjoy life on a fundamental, back-to-basics level has become a lost art. He argues that the joy of living and the joy of playing as we did as children is essential for optimum physical and psychological health.

For busy women, the value of elemental pleasures such as reading novels, taking up photography as a hobby, or taking acting lessons is unquestionable. Otherwise, why is it that Type-A workaholics have high blood pressure, poor long-term romantic relationships, and ulcers, despite the fact that they claim to love work? And why is it that once we begin to balance the lives of these executives, giving them more of the non-achievement pleasures in life, their health suddenly and dramatically improves?

Now that you know what your happiness quotient is, let's look at a system designed to provide more equilibrium to your life. As your lifestyle becomes more balanced, the power of food over your life will diminish accordingly.

Chapter 17

THE LIFESTYLE BALANCING MODULE: DAYS 11 AND 12

How Not to Put All Your Eggs in One Basket

Now that you have examined your obligations and pleasures in life, let's go about the task of expanding your pleasures to increase your happiness quotient. What new activities would bring you more satisfaction? And where are you going to find the time to fit them into your life? We must be careful not to add more and more to your daily schedule without rearranging things a bit. The goal certainly is not to make your life *more* hectic and complicated!

Turning Off Your Internal Critic

All of us have had moments when we have thought, "I really need more out of life. I must do more for *me* on a regular basis. I treat other people better than I do myself. I always come last in my priorities." But what holds us back from change? Why don't we allow ourselves more of the pleasures in life?

We have identified six false beliefs that may be holding you back. See if any of these apply to you:

I can't do more for myself because . . .

1. . . . if I really start enjoying myself, I'll begin to lose control of my life and I will not fulfill my obligations.

2. . . . having fun means that I am self-indulgent and not working up to my potential.

3. . . . having fun is non-productive and wastes time.

4. . . . I don't deserve it.

5. . . . I don't have the time.

6. . . . I can't think of anything I really enjoy doing.

For the time being, put all of these beliefs out of your mind and take our word for it that they are all *untrue*. Or there may be other reasons you use to hold yourself back from enjoying life. Write these in your notebook. Then realize they are untrue as well—because *the truth is, you deserve to enjoy your life.*

You will be gaining a healthier and more balanced control over all aspects of your life by following the exercises for Days 11 and 12. *Don't evaluate your self-worth in terms of how much time and energy you put into your obligations.*

Having fun is unquestionably self-indulgent and non-productive. But that's what pleasures are all about. It's okay to be self-indulgent some of the time. You needn't evaluate everything you do in terms of its productivity. You achieve so much in your life that you must balance it with activities that you do simply for the pleasure of doing them. You don't even have to be good at them! Think about that.

> **Crucial Fact #30**
> You can enjoy a leisure-time activity even though you don't accomplish anything by doing it.

For example, you might love to sing but, in spite of your best efforts, you can't carry a tune in a bucket. Should you give up singing? Of course not! Sing to your heart's delight if it brings you pleasure. Don't stop to evaluate your performance. You don't have to be good at it. Have friends or loved ones ever told you that you are overly critical, especially of yourself? There are times when self-judgment is useful, such as with your family or in your career. There are other times when it is very harmful. It's important to know when to turn off your internal critic.

Why not treat yourself with at least as much respect as you do those around you? You put a lot of effort into your life. You more than deserve some real pleasure each day. In fact, pleasure is not only necessary, it is *imperative* in order to conquer the SWEET Syndrome once and for all.

Although you are a busy person, pursuing many worthwhile activities, being "busy" can also serve as a great excuse for not taking good care of yourself. If you are too busy to balance your pleasures with your obligations, you are not to be admired for being such a dedicated person, you are to be pitied for being such a poor manager of your time. We are going to change all that.

One reason to do more for yourself today is that life is shorter than you think. This may seem trite, but it is dramatically true. We'll never forget Mildred, the 52-year-old owner of a small chain of retail stores in the Midwest. For her entire working life, Mildred's career came first, before personal pleasure. She and her husband, an insurance salesman in Indianapolis, dreamed of the day they would retire at an early age to live on Hilton Head Island.

"I'll be able to enjoy my life when we retire. Until then I'm going to work, work, work," she would say.

Sadly, one month after Mildred and her husband moved to Hilton Head she suffered a massive stroke. It has left her unable to speak and completely paralyzed on her left side. While her life is not over by any means, we cannot help but think that she waited too long to begin enjoying life.

Crucial Fact #31
Life is short.

There is an old Chinese proverb that translates as, "People in the West are always getting ready to live." It's time to stop "getting ready" and start living! Once you balance your life with pleasures as well as obligations, your life will feel richer, and you will have taken a major step out of the Smart Woman's Excessive Eating Trap.

The What if . . . Game

The first step in balancing your life is to take a careful look at how you currently are living. The *What if . . . Game*, below, can be useful in this regard.

Ask yourself the following question and give the answer serious consideration:

> What if your day-to-day life were exactly the same as it is now for the rest of your life? Would you look back on your life and say, "I have led a very satisfying and full life. If I had it to do over again, I would live my life in exactly the same way?"

Give these questions deep thought. Don't base your answer on how much you feel you will accomplish in life, but rather on how *happy* you would be living your life as it is *now* forever.

If you're like most people, and if you are being honest with yourself, you'll probably speculate that your life could be better.

Life must be more than simply putting in your time each day. There should be a joy to your life. When all is said and done, the good times should outweigh the bad ones.

Crucial Fact #32
"Measurement of life should be proportioned rather to the intensity of the experience than to its actual length."
—Thomas Hardy

Let's take this game one step further. Turn to a blank sheet in your notebook and answer the following question:

What if you were told by your doctor that you had only one year to live? If this were the case, what pleasures would you seek in the next 12 months?

Include "major" pleasures such as taking an extended trip to the Orient, as well as minor ones such as reading a particular book that you've been meaning to read for a long time. You might also consider increasing the frequency of pleasurable activities that you do only every once in a while.

Another area of pleasurable activities includes all those things that you've always wanted to do but have never done. Think of all those pleasures that are in the "one-day-I'm-going-to-take-time-to-do-that" category.

Write down every pleasure you can think of. *Don't stop to evaluate any of them.* Keep brainstorming until you can't think of anything else. Remember, approach this task from the standpoint of having only one year to live.

One further point. The pleasures you list can be as practical or as frivolous as you like. The point is to write as many items as possible.

The *What if . . . Game* is a great way to generate a long list of pleasures from which you can choose a few to increase your happiness quotient. Mary, a 28-year-old executive recruiter from New York City, was very successful in her career and was totally committed to her work, as well as to her husband and two children. She rarely did anything to give herself pleasure. Mary consulted us after she had gained 20 pounds because her eating habits had gotten completely out of control. In addition, she was beginning to lose interest in her work.

196

To look for ways to better balance her life, Mary compiled the following list of pleasures in response to our "What if . . ," question.

Mary's List of Pleasurable Activities

Go for a ride in a hot-air balloon
Learn to fly a plane
Write a mystery novel
Visit Tahiti
Go white water rafting
Ice skate
Go on an archeological dig
Drive a race car
Design a line of clothes for businesswomen
Take acting lessons
Learn to speak Italian
Collect Impressionist paintings
Go on an Outward Bound trip
Play racquetball
Learn more about astronomy
Collect and listen to classical music
Take an art history course
Go dancing
Telephone or write to old friends
Take singing lessons
Take up bicycling as a hobby
Take a cycling vacation in Europe
Become an amateur portrait photographer
Watch more old movies

As you can see, Mary assembled quite a long list of possible pleasures. Now, if Mary looked at her list from a purely practical standpoint, she would probably hear herself saying, "I could never find the time to do even a small portion of these. Besides, what would people think if someone like me took singing or acting lessons?"

When you look over your own list, *turn off this practical voice. This is the voice that seeks homeostasis and doesn't want you to change. This voice is your enemy.*

Post this list in a prominent place in your home. Anytime you think of a new pleasure, write it down. Always consider pleasurable activities in terms of the short run, as if you had only one year left in your life. Otherwise, you will forget that life is short and you will continue to postpone changing your life for another month, a year, or even a decade.

Establishing a Three-Point Plan of Action

Now that you have a long list of potential pleasures (you should have at least 15), it's time to choose one or two to start with. Start out by determining which ones you might enjoy the most right now, and which ones will fit most comfortably into your life.

Carefully look over your list and decide which two or three could be put into practice immediately.

> *Action #1:* *In the next 48 hours, take steps to initiate three activities on your list.*

For example, if you wanted to take lessons in photography, your first step might simply be to inquire about lessons—who offers them, when they are scheduled, and how much they cost. No commitments at first; just inquiry. The idea is to take things one step at a time. You might even buy a book on photography or talk to someone at your local camera shop to see if this is a hobby you would enjoy. Think of these initial efforts as sampling a few activities to see if you're going to enjoy participating fully in them.

Remember, *getting started* with important changes in your life is often the most difficult part. Don't hesitate.

Mary (whose pleasurable activities were listed above) found this gradual approach to change very helpful. All she was required to do for Action #1 was to:

1. Telephone a local private air service to inquire about the cost and time required to take flying lessons.

2. Check out an art history book at the local library and telephone a nearby college regarding adult-education art history courses.

3. Plan an outing with her husband to a night spot for an evening of dancing.

Action #2: Choose one of the three activities that would fit most easily into your current schedule.

If none of them would fit easily, sample others on your list until you come up with one that looks like it would be an easy fit. Try to choose an activity that you will be able to participate in on a regular basis, at least once a week. For example, Mary chose to take an art history course that met one night a week and that, fortunately, was starting in two weeks.

Action #3:   Reserve a specific time for your activity.

As you think about your schedule for the week, don't say, "I'll fit my pleasure in sometime, but I'm not sure exactly when." Consider this pleasure time to be as essential as any other time in your life. Think of it as scheduling an appointment as you would any other—an appointment that cannot be broken.

Using either your notebook or your appointment calendar, write a list of all the times that you have available for these activities. Choose times that are likely to be free each week. Avoid times during which you might have distractions or even periodic responsibilities.

In Mary's case, her art history class met on Tuesday evenings, a time that was free for her. Although she sometimes brought work home to complete in the evening, she decided never to do this on Tuesday as long as her college course was in session. She even decided to refuse all but the most special social invitations on Tuesday evenings for the duration of her course.

Once your pleasure time has been set, *only* a major catastrophe should change it. *Demand* this time of yourself. Don't allow yourself or anyone else to whittle away at it. If something at work or in your family life comes along to interfere with that time, think first about finding a substitute time for your career or family. *You* are important.

Taking your pleasure time seriously is very, very important if you are ever to take charge of your life and get control of the SWEET Syndrome.

Fitting Pleasures into Your Busy Schedule

Many people find that as they add more pleasurable activities to their lives, they have difficulty finding enough time to adequately handle both their obligations and their pleasures. Time constraints and poor time management can be your greatest obstacles to success, *if you let them*.

If your obligations already take a great deal of your time, you should not simply add more hours to your overcrowded schedule by getting up earlier, going to bed later, or skipping other daily routines. We suggest you find time by looking at ways you can accomplish more in less time or delegate authority to someone else.

Two of the best ways to find more time are to *compartmentalize* and to *delegate*. Compartmentalizing is the practice of scheduling only one activity during a particular time and not allowing any other activity to interfere. For example, you might decide to respond to correspondence from 9:00 A.M. to 10:00 A.M., meet with your associates on a certain project from 10:00 A.M. to 11:00 A.M., seclude yourself for creative thinking from 11:00 to 11:45, and return telephone calls during the rest of the morning. Compartmentalizing activities is one thing, but making sure distractions do not interfere is another. You do need to screen out interruptions as much as possible. Otherwise, you will not finish your correspondence because you are taking non-crucial telephone calls, or you will not have your creative time because a colleague wishes to talk to you during that time. Your time is extremely valuable. Answer the telephone call later and ask your colleague to wait until the afternoon to meet with you. Otherwise, you will be staying late to finish your obligations and will therefore miss out on your scheduled pleasure time after work.

Delegation is also a necessary tool of time management. You must learn to delegate both career and family responsibilities in order to give yourself necessary pleasure time. *The main impediment to delegating appropriately is none other than yourself.*

You may hesitate to delegate because delegation means giving up control. Worse yet, you might delegate to someone who doesn't do the job nearly as well as you could! (That means giving up perfectionism.)

Have you ever heard yourself say, "By the time I explain the correct way of doing this to someone else, I could have done it myself." This might be true the first time, but after that, they will be able to do the task without your assistance. Be content with the fact that not everyone will accomplish every task just as you do or even as well as you do. So what? You are not going to be irresponsible about delegating duties. If it's not a crucial duty, what difference does it make that it was not done your way? Relax and do a little more mental reconditioning. If this continues to be a problem, go back to the Cognitive Change Module and do some work with your notebook and tape recorder on this issue.

In your notebook, write down two career, family, or personal responsibilities. Avoid choosing very crucial activities or ones that only you personally can accomplish. Under each activity, list possible family members, friends, subordinates, or co-workers to whom you could delegate this responsibility, either all or some of the time. Also write ways in which you might approach them about this matter and any resistance you might encounter.

Depending on your work situation, you might have to request scheduling changes from your boss. For example, in order to attend her Tuesday class, Mary asked the manager of her firm to allow her to leave an hour earlier that evening in exchange for her coming in an hour earlier the next morning. She also asked her husband to take charge of the children and all other household duties that night. With respect to personal chores, you may decide to hire someone to help you in order to free up your time. Or consider doing those chores less often.

Now that you have thought through this process of delegation, it's time for action. In the next 48 hours, delegate both of the responsibilities listed in your notebook to someone else. Whatever you have to do to make this happen, *do it,* and do it in the next two days.

Putting It All Together

Turn to a clean page in your notebook and make out a sample weekly schedule for yourself. The first activities that should go into your schedule are your pleasure times. Start out with one and add more as the weeks go on. You should have at least as many pleasures as necessary to bring your happiness quotient into the 25 to 40 range.

After your pleasure times are marked out, add all of your obligations. Make the schedule work.

You may have to rework your schedule from time to time to make sure everything fits. You may even decide that one or two of your pleasures are not cracked up to what you thought they would be. That's okay. Just choose one or two more from your list and start over. Stay flexible.

Before you know it, you'll be enjoying your new *balanced* lifestyle. Your life will be richer and fuller. This fact, combined with the techniques you put into practice in preceding chapters, will gradually erase any remaining negative behavior toward food.

Chapter 18

FIFTY HELPFUL HINTS FOR MAXIMIZING YOUR MASTERY OVER FOOD

Now that you have worked your way through the Hilton Head Program, you are in a much better position to implement some specific techniques designed to tackle the work-related eating situations described in Chapter 3. Your New Willpower will make it easier for you to implement these tips in your daily life.

All of these techniques are based in common sense. Some of them may seem obvious. Our experience, however, is that common sense is not always common practice. The most effective techniques are generally the simplest ones.

Let's take a look at each of these work situations and what can be done to improve your control when exposed to them.

Remaining Effective During Business Meals

• If you have a choice, select a restaurant that caters to your taste and whose menu you know. Choose restaurants that serve nutritious, healthy food. Keep a list in your workbook or diary of restaurants that cater to your needs.

• Make up your mind before you even enter the restaurant what you are going to eat. Keep a record of the meals that you have enjoyed at various restaurants. This will make your planning and meal-ordering easier. If you are uncertain about what is available at a particular restaurant, call beforehand to inquire about the menu. Try to order first so you are not influenced by other people's choices.

• Ask the waiter how items are cooked and what the sauces, dressings, or stuffings are made from. Do not be shy about asking for food to be prepared in a special way, broiled for example, or about asking that dressings be served on the side. Many people take their own dressings to restaurants. If you are assertive in this way, chances are that your colleagues/clients will respect you for being direct and getting what you want. They will interpret your behavior as being resourceful and positive rather than finicky and negative.

• Portion control is very important. Many people make a good nutritional choice, but then eat too much of it. It reminds us of the old cartoon in which a rather overweight lady looks to the waiter and orders, "three of the diet special." Portion control is particularly important at restaurants where you may feel some pressure to "get your money's worth." Resist this thought and watch those portions.

• One of the most difficult times in a restaurant occurs when you are waiting for your food to arrive. You are hungry and surrounded by food. Avoid the bread and butter by asking the waitress to take it from the table, or push it out of reach. Order a sugar-free soft drink or some sparkling

208

water. This is an ideal time to concentrate on business rather than food.

• Decide ahead of time, whether or not you are going to drink alcohol. Know exactly what drinks (alcoholic or otherwise) you are going to order. Remember that alcohol poses several threats to the person who wishes to control her eating.

Alcohol contains "empty" calories that have no nutritional value. You lead a busy life that can drain you of energy. All your calories should be nutritional rather than "empty." If you are on a low-calorie plan (fewer than 1000 calories per day), alcohol should always be seen as an extra to a low-calorie plan, not part of it. Be forewarned that through its effect on the lining of your stomach, alcohol stimulates appetite.

Alcohol also has a disinhibiting effect. As we have said before, your best intentions might well dissolve after you have had a couple of drinks.

In addition, alcohol's relaxing effect is relatively short-lived. In fact, once the initial effect has worn off, you are likely to feel more tense than you did before drinking.

It has become much more acceptable to limit alcohol consumption or eschew it altogether. The decision to curtail alcohol intake draws more respect than derision in our health-conscious society.

• Whatever you decide to do, *be decisive.* Remember, it is the way you behave *rather* than what you eat that will create the strongest impression on other people. Do not be defensive or focus on the issue of food or your choices. Do not make excuses about having medical conditions or being on special diets. You have an absolute right to eat what you want. You do not have to justify your eating behavior to anyone except yourself.

Crucial Fact #33
The medium is the message. How you conduct yourself is far more important than what you eat.

Using the New Willpower at Cocktail Parties

• You can minimize your exposure to the temptations of a cocktail party by arriving later and leaving early.

• Do not go to a cocktail party hungry. Have a small snack beforehand to minimize your temptation. A piece of fruit is an ideal choice for a snack that will take the edge off your hunger while giving you a boost of energy.

• Decide before you go what you are going to have to drink. If you are drinking alcohol, alternate alcoholic and soft drinks. Write your decisions in your notebook before you leave for the party to crystalize them in your own mind.

• Decide beforehand whether it is your intention to eat at the party. If you are going to eat, decide what sort of food it will be and how much of it you intend to eat. Write these decisions in your notebook, too.

• Keep away from the buffet table. Do not stand near the food unless you are deliberately trying to practice your craving-control techniques. Distance yourself from the food table as much as possible. Always do more talking than eating.

Meetings

Our clients have reported success using the following techniques to deal with meetings at which food is served.

• Try to influence the choice of food. Others in the meeting may have the same thoughts and wishes as you do and are hoping that someone will make the appropriate suggestions. Suggest a variety of food which includes some that suits your taste.

• If the meal is a buffet, take what you want on one plate. Make up your mind to make just one trip to the table. When you are finished eating, push the plate to one side or dispose of it.

• If the food is provided as a sit-down meal, make the best choices available to you. From both a weight-control and a nutritional viewpoint, the best choices are those that are low in fat. For a more detailed nutritional plan designed both for weight loss and general health maintenance, we encourage you to read *The Hilton Head Metabolism Diet* and *The Hilton Head Executive Stamina Program*.

• We strongly advocate setting calorie limits. Decide how many calories you are going to consume during the course of the day, and stick to that limit. The mental discipline of setting calorie limits, monitoring your intake, and staying within those limits, is the *most important part* of weight-watching and eating control. Whether you are trying to lose weight, maintain weight, or simply trying to eat healthily, it is important that you know what your calorie limits are, and that you monitor yourself to stay within these limits. Do not be concerned that others are watching what you eat and drink. Most people don't notice and the rest don't care.

• If the meeting is not going to last too long and there will be a chance for you to eat afterward, do not eat in the meeting itself. With your attention on the meeting and your adrenaline flowing, you are at greater risk of overeating in, rather than out, of the meeting. Depending on the timing of the meeting and your schedule, you may actually be able to eat *beforehand*. If that is the case, just make sure you don't eat beforehand *and* at the meeting!

Formal Dinners

• Where appropriate and possible, use the restaurant techniques to control the nature and the amount of food you consume. If you have no choice, eat the less-fattening foods, the carbohydrates and protein, and leave the remainder on your plate. Don't worry about justifying or drawing attention to your behavior. Simply leave what you are not eating on the side of the plate.

• Watch your alcohol intake. With waiters refilling your glass, you can easily lose track of your alcohol consumption. Ask for sparkling water such as Perrier, or non-alcoholic wines, if available.

• Depending on the circumstances, consider arriving after the meal.

On the Road

Whether for business or pleasure, traveling can be extremely stressful. If possible, organize your arrangements, packing, etc., far enough in advance so these tasks are not left to do in a rush at the last minute.

• Keep a traveling bag ready at all times. This should contain personal documents, toiletries, and other small useful travel items such as a sewing kit.

• Have a master checklist of tasks you need to complete prior to leaving. Work your way down the list systematically, giving yourself enough time to do so without having to rush. Your master checklist might include the following items:

Pick up tickets.

Confirm hotel reservations.

Check all travel documents (visas, passports, etc.).

Check all work/business documents.

Check clothes for repairs/cleaning.

Assemble toiletries, travel items (alarm clock, reading material, etc.) in one place for quick packing.

When you are finally in transit, here are some recommendations that will cut down on stress and help you monitor your eating:

• Order a "special" meal when booking your flight. A wide range of such special meals are available, including low-calorie, diabetic, kosher, low-cholesterol, low-salt, and vegetarian plates. Although you should try to establish what each of these dishes contains, that is not always easy. Some of the vegetarian dishes, for example, are high in both dairy products and calories. As a rule of thumb, however, you are always better off with a "special" meal than with the standard fare.

• If you are expecting a long wait for a connecting flight, plan your activities and meals. Take a snack, ideally some fruit, with you. Be sure that you have activities to occupy you, but make sure that paperwork is not your only pastime. Select a few pleasure activities from your list that are feasible for travel. Walking around the airport terminal while doing some people-watching will provide diversion and even help burn off a few calories.

• Do *not* drink alcohol in-flight. When combined with the pressurization of the airplane cabin, alcohol's dehydrating effect is magnified, depleting you of energy and making you more fatigued and susceptible to jet lag. You may eat foods you don't want in order to regain lost energy.

• Do not stay seated for too long a time. Periodically walk about and do some gentle stretching exercises to prevent muscle stiffness. When your muscles are not used for a long period, lactic acid accumulates and contributes to fatigue and loss of mental sharpness.

• When traveling by car, have the times when you will stop for a meal planned in advance.

• When booking hotel reservations, inquire about the

sort of restaurant facilities available. Try to get information about local restaurants in advance, either through the hotel, travel agent, travel guidebook, tourist information bureau, or Chamber of Commerce. Consider hotels that have exercise facilities, or are located where you can safely walk.

In addition to the hints above, our clients have frequently reported three other techniques that work well:

• Always have a small snack available. Typically this snack will be a piece of fruit and a cracker or some melba toast. The snack will fend off hunger for an hour or so and give you some extra energy without your having to resort to a more substantial snack or meal at an inappropriate time. Carry such snacks in the car and have one in your office as a contingency measure.

• Carry a toothbrush with you and brush your teeth immediately after you have finished your meal. Many of our clients report that the ritual of teeth cleaning and the oral freshness that results is a good antidote against further, unplanned eating.

• Remember that the few minutes spent planning your choices and anticipating the eating situation beforehand will be extremely valuable. Use visualization techniques to prepare yourself by recreating the situation in your mind and "walking" yourself through it. In this way you will be able to identify the danger points and make decisions in advance about how you will handle them. Above all, be decisive and do not be influenced by others. Put yourself firmly in charge!

Chapter
19

HOW TO
MOTIVATE YOURSELF
FOR THE REST
OF YOUR LIFE

Now that you have achieved a new Level of Mastery through the 12-day program, all you need is the motivation to maintain it. Studies show that successful people who maintain their behavior change cultivate the following traits.

Keeping Alert

The best way to maintain any new behavior is to demonstrate what psychologists call "cognitive vigilance." People who do this are constantly aware of the events and places that may be problems. They are not obsessive, but they *never stop monitoring* potential high-risk situations.

People who are successful at maintaining their behavior have devised a *range* of coping strategies. They decide ahead of time what they plan to do in a tempting situation.

The Power of Positive Thinking

It is clear, not only from research but also from our casework, that another crucial characteristic is the right attitude. Our most successful clients have been those who exhibit what experts call a "high internal locus of control." The "locus of control" is a measure of where individuals believe the control of their lives rests. If you believe that you possess the power to guide your own life and assume responsibility for yourself, you will be highly internally controlled. If you feel you have little control and that your fate rests with others (or with outside circumstances), you are externally controlled. Rethink your outlook if this is the case. You have achieved so much that you aren't giving yourself credit for! Seize your own destiny and take charge of your life!

What to Do Right When Things Go Wrong

It's a fact of life that some days are going to be easier than others, that on some occasions you will be in complete control of your eating and on others you will be less so. It is also important to realize that the difficult days do not invalidate your efforts or wipe out your progress. In fact, the way in which you deal with setbacks is absolutely crucial, because *setbacks can be a powerful source of strength.*

Let's take the case of Patti, a real estate developer from

the South. Her job involved travel, long hours, and a seemingly endless round of evening cocktail parties. She had eradicated the SWEET Syndrome by using the Hilton Head Program, and had been successfully implementing the program for five months when she ran into difficulties. After a particularly harrowing day, she found herself with a very demanding client at an evening gathering. To make matters worse, she had not eaten any lunch and was extremely hungry. She managed to hold out for a while, but before long she found herself exceeding her self-imposed alcohol limit. This made her hungrier and weakened her willpower. Her best intentions dissolved in alcohol! She ended up eating more than was necessary from the buffet table and going back for a second helping of her favorite dessert. By the time she got home she was disgusted with herself and very upset. She saw herself as "back to square one." She completely ignored all the excellent progress she had made in the previous five months and saw herself as a failure. Fortunately, she turned to the Cognitive Change Module of her notebook and used her Flexibility Thinking lists to look at the situation more objectively.

Patti's first thinking mistake was that she had not prepared herself for the eventuality of setbacks. As you'll recall from Chapter 7, the road of life is sometimes rocky! So you should not be surprised if an eating problem resurfaces *periodically*. Patti had not seriously considered this possibility and as a result was not only unprepared, but was shocked and self-critical when it happened.

Secondly, Patti fell victim to all-or-nothing thinking. To her mind she either was in complete control, or she had no control whatsoever. When she suffered a slip-up this one time, she generalized that her control had gone forever! Patti was suffering from a violation of both her vows and expectations.

Patti used the Cognitive Change Module to help herself understand that her eating episode was not a disaster. Adopting a flexible thinking pattern, she decided that it was an unfortunate incident, but one that could be learned from. Difficult circumstances had conspired to put enormous pressure on her to eat. She learned that she had not been fully prepared for this situation, and that once it had occurred, it revealed unrealistic expectations about herself that revolved around her notion of forever having perfect control. She used the incident to mount an argument against this Thinking Mistake.

Crucial Fact #34
Circumstances will sometimes conspire to challenge your implementation of the program. A slip-up does not mean that you have "relapsed" or that your previous progress counts for nothing.

How to Stay on the Program When You Want to Get Off

Donna is a paralegal working for a large Atlanta law firm. She embarked on our program to achieve greater food control and a more balanced lifestyle. On returning home, she enthusiastically continued the program of assignments described in this book. After a month or so at home, however, her involvement in the program began to lessen. No major life changes or unusual events occurred during this period to create a setback situation. Her workload had increased, but not to the point of seriously stressing her.

When we contacted Donna as part of our follow-up, she told us that she put the program into practice whenever she thought about it, but not in any consistent manner. Donna described how at a party or some other business-related event she would "happen to find herself" eating foods that she consciously had no intention of eating. She would "happen to find herself" in her favorite delicatessen. She spoke almost as if she had been teleported there! Donna's unconscious was telling her what she could not easily admit to herself—she had lost motivation.

Why do people lose motivation? Remember what we mentioned earlier in the book: Willpower and self-management are skills that can be *learned*. There is nothing magical about them. They are produced and maintained consciously. Sometimes, when you are busy or preoccupied, you may find them pushed to the back of your mind.

Also, motivation fluctuates in response to your perception of the costs and benefits of doing any activity. We have developed what we call the Willpower Balance Sheet to help you keep sight of the rewards of the Program.

The Willpower Balance Sheet. Let's take the case of Donna described above. Early in the program, her motivation to continue the program and do the assignments looked like this on her Willpower Balance Sheet:

Pros

I will feel better.
I will lose weight.
I will look better.
I will be more in control of my life.
I will be more efficient at work.
I will have a better social life.
I will have more self-respect.

Cons

I will have to expend effort.
Initially it will take some time.
I might fail.

After Donna reached a certain level on the program, many of the "pros" either had been achieved or became available only over the long term. Donna had lost some weight and felt better physically and mentally. Initially, people remarked on this difference, but once her new look was accepted as the norm, the comments and compliments began to taper off. The more long-term benefits of the program receded in Donna's mind. (As you learned in Chapter 6, behavior is generally guided by short-term consequences.)

At this stage, Donna's Willpower Balance Sheet looked like this:

Pros

I will have more control over my eating.

Cons

I will have to expend effort.
I might fail.

Understand that a Willpower Balance Sheet does not reflect a logical reality; it is merely your *perception* of the consequences of doing any particular action.

To keep your motivation high and to reduce the risk of setbacks, consider some of the tips we gave to Donna.

Never let the benefits of the program slip from your view. You can ensure that this does not happen by adopting the following four techniques:

1. In your notebook, make a personal list of all the advantages you continue to receive from this program. Keep that list in a prominent place and refer to it regularly, adding items as they occur.

2. Use some positive imagery to reinforce the above-mentioned advantages. Imagine yourself as having achieved these goals. See yourself as fitter, healthier, more empowered in areas of life that are meaningful to you.

3. Reward yourself for staying with the program. These rewards should be based on your *behavior* rather than on anything else (such as weight loss). The rewards should *not* be in the form of food,

even "healthy" foods, since this can lead to food being used as a comforter, a misperception of the function of food that underpins many eating difficulties. Give yourself other treats, like books, audio tapes, or clothes. Keep the rewards short-term, perhaps contingent on your performance every other week. In that way you will receive regular reinforcement for your efforts. Donna began rewarding herself like this after her consultation with us:

Weeks 1 and 2	Stayed on plan	Bought two new audio cassettes
Weeks 3 and 4	Stayed on plan	Bought book
Weeks 5 and 6	Deviated slightly	No reward
Weeks 7 and 8	Stayed on plan	Saved money for new shoes
Weeks 9 and 10	Stayed on plan	Bought shoes

4. Spend some time each week reviewing your progress and planning for the week ahead. Set your behavioral goals and reward yourself where appropriate. Anticipate the "high risk" situations that might arise during the next week and devise appropriate coping strategies. Use visualization to practice your response to these potentially challenging situations. Donna called these enjoyable planning sessions "a meeting with myself."

The Confidence Restorers

For a real boost, follow the five-part plan we gave to Donna.

First, we asked Donna to *reaffirm her goals* by writing down her reasons for wanting to implement the program. Secondly, Donna reread the Cognitive Change Module, using it to identify any *destructive thoughts that were obstructing her progress*. Thirdly, we suggested to Donna that she tackle some of the more challenging "Close Encounter" assignments on the Craving Control Ladder. This she did, retracing her steps up the ladder, ending with the Tasting Exercises. Fourth, Donna *reacquainted herself with the Lifestyle Balancing Module,* revising it where necessary. Lastly, we encouraged Donna to *review her goal sheet weekly* and even to carry her list with her in her wallet so she would see it each time she opened her handbag. We encouraged her to review this list whenever she experienced some desire to overindulge in a craved food, or when a difficult eating situation arose. These steps, combined with the system of short-term rewards she devised and her 15-minute "meeting with myself" each week, helped Donna to regain her enthusiasm and thus her motivation. She continues today to lead a well-balanced life free of the SWEET Syndrome.

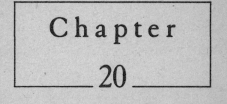

Chapter 20

A FINAL WORD

Now that we have outlined the Hilton Head Program, don't hestitate one minute in getting started! This treatment strategy *will* work for you.

Negative eating habits happen to many women. It is precisely because you lead a busy, rewarding life that you are so at risk for this problem. It comes with the territory. You, like everyone else, are human and, at times, in need of help. We hope you have found it here. We know that you will be able to use this program successfully. We have faith in you!

Ours is the only plan that is specifically developed with your lifestyle and personality in mind. All the diets and nutritional education in the world are not as tailor-made to your needs as this program is. The promise of this program is a life in which you are effective in managing all aspects of your involvements: career, family, relationships with friends, *and* healthy eating.

Now is the time for action—positive action that not only will change your eating habits, but could change your life.

This new life awaits you. It is just around the corner. You will have put the SWEET Syndrome behind you once and for all!

We welcome your letters and questions. If you would like more information about the Hilton Head Health Institute or the program offered in this book, please write to:

> Hilton Head Health Institute
> Department X
> P.O. Box 7138
> Hilton Head Island, SC 29938-7138

INDEX

233

W